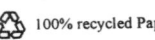

BLACKBURN IN TIMES GONE BY

BLACKBURN IN TIMES GONE BY

Compiled by

Jim Halsall

Landy Publishing
1998

© Copyright in this book is held by
United Newspapers and by Jim Halsall.

Landy Publishing

ISBN 1 872895 39 5

British Library in Cataloguing Publication Data.
A catalogue record of this book is available from the British Library.

Layout by Mike Clarke, 01254 395848

07543427

Printed by

Landy Publishing have also published:

The Blackburn Samaritan by Trevor Moore
A Blackburn Miscellany edited by Bob Dobson
Blackburn & Darwen A Century Ago by Alan Duckworth
Bits of Old Blackburn by Shaw & Hulme, illus. by Chas. Haworth
Blackburn's Old Inns by George Miller
Blackburn's Shops at the Turn of the Century by Matthew Cole
Blackburn's West End by Matthew Cole
Threads of Lancashire Life by Winnie Bridges
A Lancashire Look by Benita Moore
The Really Lancashire Book edited by Bob Dobson
Lancashire, this, that an't'other by Doris Snape

A full list is available from:

Landy Publishing
'Acorns' 3 Staining Rise, Staining, Blackpool, FY3 0BU
Tel/Fax: 01253 895678

...Table of Contents...

PREFACE

This book began as an off-shoot from my hobby of researching Blackburn's trams, an interest of mine for the best part of the last thirty years.

Whilst searching for information amongst old newspapers, I often came across important local history articles, many of which were on micro-film. Some of the micro-film reels were in negative form, and in order to retrieve the photographs, I had to develop a technique for reprinting them, and so made suitable modifications to my photographic enlarger.

These articles first appeared in *The Blackburn Times*, which ceased publication on 8th July 1982; the paper's photographic collection disappeared without trace. Those reproduced here have come from Blackburn Library's microfilm copies of the newspaper. They start at 1890, and I have made 1939 my cut-off point. Most of these photographs are historically rare if not unique, and this galvanised me to create the book as an historical record for future generations to enjoy.

The articles have been collated in chronological order as published to allow the reader to travel back in time and yet come forward as the articles are read. The dated source of the articles and photos is given with the heading. The reader has to remember that when the text refers to "the present", it means the date of publication. In some cases, I have added a map to give today's readers an indication of where a particular street or property once was.

This has been, for me, a most enjoyable trip down Memory Lane. I hope that my efforts to recover lost pieces of Blackburn history proves to be as interesting and enjoyable to you as it has been for me.

I want to acknowledge my thanks to my long- suffering wife Marie, who has had to put up with mounds of manuscript sheets and drying photographic prints that sometimes threatened to engulf the whole house; Ian Sutton and all the girls at Blackburn Reference Library, who have given me help and guidance at all times. They are a staff to be proud of. I thank Ian too for writing an introduction; June Huntingdon of Accrington for her help and encouragement; Alan Parkin of Accrington for help in the technique for retrieving the photographs; Ray Smith for the loan of his *Blackburn Times* banners and notepaper; Steven Owens for a letterheading: Ken Hampshire for help along the way; Ben Keller of Burnley for the sketches included in the turnpike article, as the photos in the original article were not suitable for reproducing; Margaret Crabtree for the additional information about Shorrock Fold; Andy Willetts for his help in guiding me through the pitfalls and brickwalls associated with learning my way around the wondrous world of the PC at the tender age of sixty; the Lancashire regional editor of United Newspapers, Neil Hodgkinson for permission to reproduce the articles and photos from the *Blackburn Times*; to the journalists and photographers of the *Blackburn Times* who created the contents of this book in the first place; lastly, I dedicate this book to the memory of my grandfather, William Smith, who was a well known photographer of Blackburn in times gone by.

Jim Halsall
Spring 1998

THE BLACKBURN TIMES.

FOREWORD

Jim recently cornered me in the Library and with great bubbling enthusiasm proceeded to lecture me on how addictive the old Blackburn Newspapers are, *"once you start reading through them you just can't stop yourself"*. Of course when you are used to handling them on a daily basis you tend to treat them as just another *"tool of the trade"*, however I must confess that whilst I always knew that they were a rich source of written local history information I had seriously underestimated them as such a prime source of illustrative material.

Although the Library has an extensive collection of photographs of Blackburn, many of the ones illustrated here will only have been seen by people prepared to search through the old copies of *The Blackburn Times*. Jim has put together a personal collection of these illustrations along with the relevant article or report that accompanied each one on the day it appeared in the newspaper.

"The last decade has seen a great change to the appearance of many of Blackburn's streets. One by one the older portions have been destroyed to make way for new buildings, until the Blackburn of today would scarcely be recognised by a visitor who had been absent for a period of ten years."

Sounds familiar? What you may be interested to know is that the above comment comes not from a newspaper editorial of today but from words accompanying an article in a local newspaper of 1904! It is interesting to note that many of the buildings shown here have now disappeared as a result of the demolition of the Victorian town centre during the numerous redevelopment phases.

Blackburn's cotton legacy, from economic transformation and rapid growth to the decline of the textile industry has been well documented in depth elsewhere. What this book shows are some of the lesser known landmarks that once made up Blackburn's ever changing skyline. Look at the old buildings on Church Street, King Street or Darwen Street, read about the Smithy that was on the site of our present day Library, the starting of the Mill Hill clock or the rope shop on Church Street.

I am sure that anyone who has an interest in the history of the town will find this book as fascinating as I did and that it evokes memories of Blackburn's heritage. Even as I am writing this I realise I could be sat either on the corner of Thunder Alley or directly below the picturesque dome of the Co-operative building!

Ian Sutton

Blackburn Times

REFUGE ASSURANCE OFFICES
May 17th 1890

No town in England, perhaps, contributes so much money in proportion to its size in the shape of industrial assurance as does the town of Blackburn, and one indication of the hold this class of assurance has on the working people of this town is seen in the handsome suite of offices recently erected in Ainsworth Street by Mr. James Wilcock, district superintendent of the Refuge Assurance Company.

These offices, a view of which is included in this article, are to be opened for the transaction of business on Monday, when the Company will move locations from Montague Street to the neighbourhood of St. John's Church.

For some years accommodation has been found in Montague Street, where some property was purchased and adapted to office purposes, but the rapid growth of the business rendered the present accommodation totally inadequate.

The new building is of considerable size, and is erected of stone and brickwork. The front is faced with Yorkshire parpoints with Yorkshire stone dressings, a considerable amount of ornamental work being introduced. It is situated at that part of Ainsworth Street opposite to the lower end of Richmond Terrace, close to the east end of St. John's Church. The whole of the work, including fittings and furniture, has been carried out from the designs, and under the supervision of Messrs. Stones and Gradwell, architects, Richmond-terrace.

Primitive Methodist Day and Sunday Schools,
Cedar St. and St. James Road. Blackburn

J S White ⎫ Circuit
W Spedding ⎭ Ministers

Simpson & Duckworth, Architects
Richmond Chambers, Blackburn

CEDAR STREET & ST. JAMES METHODIST SCHOOLS

October 11ᵗʰ 1890

This afternoon Mr. W. D. Coddington, M.P., will lay the foundation stone of new day and Sunday school premises which the Primitive Methods are erecting at the junction of St. James's Road and Cedar Street.

The present chapel was built about 20 years ago at a cost of £4,000, and day schools were erected at a later period at an additional cost of £3,000.

The responsibility for the initiation of the new schools rested on the trustees of the Oxford Street Chapel, who, about 18 months ago, secured sufficient land for the purpose, and voted £200 from the Oxford-street Trust as the nucleus of a building fund. Land was secured on which to build a

chapel, as well as the proposed commodious schools, but at present only the schools will be proceeded with. If the mission grows as is anticipated, the chapel will follow. Messrs. Simpson and Duckworth, Richmond Terrace, are the architects for the work, which is to cost £1,347. The contract for the whole of it has been let to Mr. Jas. Whittaker, of Blackburn, who has sub-let the joiner's work to Mr. James Sharples. The plot of land, including the site of a new church, contains 2195 square yards.

The school will consist of a mixed department for 214 scholars, with three classrooms divided from the main room by glazed sliding partitions, and an infant department and classroom to each section.

ST. PAUL'S CHURCH
December 20th 1890

When first built, in 1791-2, the fabric consisted of nave and steeple. There were four entrances, the principal ones being respectively on the north and south sides, between the fourth and fifth windows[reckoning towards the east], and the minor entrance to the west gable, on each side of the tower. Only one of these remains, and that is but little used. The new vestry, to be seen on the left of the engraving, takes the place of one of the minor entrances.

The footpath shown in the engraving leads direct from the churchyard gate to the walled-up south entrance. On both sides of the church traces of the walled-up ancient doorways are to be seen. There were always ten windows on each side, as at present.

The principal structural alteration that was ever made in the church was that made in 1866-7, when the vestry was built at the south-west corner, followed by the erection of the chancel and entrance halls at the east end. The appearance of the church was improved both internally and externally by this alteration, and the accommodation considerably augmented.

One of the present main entrances is shown on the extreme right of the picture, the other being on the opposite side of the chancel. The graveyard, now closed for burials, lies mainly on the south-side of the church, and the path shown in the picture leads through it from Nab Lane. The path extends all the way round the church, and the gate on the other side in St.Paul Street is the one most used.

MANCHESTER & COUNTY BANK
January 31ˢᵗ 1891

The engraving represents the new premises of the Manchester and County Bank, which will be opened for business on Monday next, The bank is built on the commanding site of the old one, overlooking the Market. It was in the year 1862 that the Manchester and County Bank was incorporated, and two years later the Blackburn branch was opened in the substantial premises, belonging to the Feildens of Witton Park.

The County Club, which occupied the upper storey of the old premises, will now have accommodation in the new premises, but the Witton Estate Offices, which were also located over the old bank, have been permanently removed.

The new bank is the property of a company called the Manchester and County Bank, Limited, and it stands on a plot of land at the corner of King William Street and New Market Street, The main entrance is in King William Street, by a handsome doorway, flanked by granite jambs and head. The contract for the whole of the building has been executed by Messrs. Robert, Neill and Sons, of Manchester; the fittings by Messrs. Simpson and Duckworth, architects, of Blackburn, have acted as building superintendents. The whole of the works have been designed and carried out under the direction of Messrs. Mills and Murgatroyd, architects, of Manchester.

THE OLD FOXHOUSE
April 11ᵗʰ 1891

Close to the Preston New Road there lies a little old cottage with which originated the well known place-name, Foxhouse. It is said to have derived the name from the killing of a fox in the vicinity by a number of local huntsmen.

The sketch in this article shows the pretty little cottage, which, though on its last legs, is still occupied. It is now so hemmed in with modern property that it has lost its ancient beauty, and nobody ever dreams of nowadays going on a picnic party to the Foxhouse as they did when our fathers and grandfathers were children. The pleasant gardens that formerly surrounded it are entirely gone now.

The Foxhouse, the Fox and Grapes, and the Fox Delph, are all on the estate of Lady Whitehead, and a generation ago the whole of the Gawthorpe section of the Bank estate from the Foxhouse to the top of Revidge was one extensive farm, farmed under Lady Whitehead by one person, Betty Dewhurst.

Above the High School and Lower Bank there was not a single house on Preston new road in 1884 before reaching the Fox and Grapes; but the Foxhouse occupied a prominent place below the line of the road on the left. The cottage is shown quite clearly on the 1884 Ordnance Survey Map, Sheet 62, 6 inches to a mile scale.

KENDAL STREET WESLEYAN CHAPEL

November 21st 1891

Very shortly the body of Wesleyans worshipping at Kendal Street Chapel will have an edifice more suited to their requirements, as the trustees are about to enter upon the erection of a handsome and commodious chapel in Altom Street, and adjoining the present chapel.

It was in the early 1870s that the Methodist body commenced a mission at Kendal Street, and the premises now used for religious purposes has been in existence for 18 years. At present there are 340 scholars enrolled on the books, with an average attendance of 270. As the services are crowded, it has become imperative to undertake the important task of building a new edifice. It is estimated that the cost will amount to about £1,000, and a large sum has already been raised by the members of the congregation who a few weeks ago promoted a successful bazaar in aid of their object.

The chapel is to be erected on a freehold plot of land which adjoins the present school. The chapel will have an imposing appearance, and the structure will be of brick with stone dressings, red pressed bricks being used for the exterior. The roof will be covered with blue slates.

LOCAL MONUMENTS OF THE TURNPIKE DAYS
April 18ᵗʰ & 25ᵗʰ 1908

In 1871 there were toll houses every six or eight miles in most parts of the country, landowners and others whose property main roads passed combining to erect toll gates for raising funds to keep the roads in repair. Under the Highways Act of 1878, however a large number of turnpike roads were turned into what are now known as main roads, the responsibility for which was thrown upon the county or other highway authority, and under the Local Government Act of 1888 the toll bar system in Great Britain was ended. Bridge tolls survive however in some places.

Sketch No.1 is of *Harwood Bar*, at the junction of the road from Great Harwood with that from Accrington, to Whalley. It then served as a county Police Station.

Sketch No. 2 represents a building which will be familiar to Blackburn people, it is the old *Craven Heifer Bar*, at the junction of the Whalley Old Road and Whalley New Road, and in April 1908, the frontage was rebuilt to form up to date shop premises, and the sketch is of the building just after the alterations had been carried out in that year.

The cottage shown in sketch No. 3 will be better known to East Lancashire people. It was in the Turnpike days called *Portfield Bar*, and stood at the point where the road from Whalley forks on the one side to Burnley and on the other to Harwood and Accrington.

The 4th sketch is of *Abbott Clough Gate Bar* and was situated not far from the Mother Red Cap Inn, on the right hand side of the tram route from Blackburn to Accrington. There was formerly a stone arch over the front, but this was blown down early in the century. The house however, still intruded on the road as in former times, and it was demolished in 1935. *(See separate article in this book on page 75)*

Harwood Bar

Craven Heifer Bar

Drawn by Ben Keller

Portfield Bar

Abbott Clough Gate Bar

Drawn by Ben Keller

Oaks Bar

Wiswell Bar

Sketch 5 is of **Oaks Bar**, which stood on the Longsight road at the point where it crossed by the road from Wilpshire and Ribchester, an ancient Roman road.

The last sketch No. 6 is the *Wiswell Bar*, and was situated at Whalley, near where the Clitheroe main road gives off the by way to Wiswell and Pendleton.

In 1908 most of the other toll houses in this district have disappeared, though the cottage still remains at the foot of Brockholes Brow, which controlled the dues for the use of the Halfpenny Bridge on Preston New Road. The Billinge, Windmill, and Five Barred Gate bars no longer remain. The Billinge bar was superseded by the one at Shackerly when Blackburn was incorporated. There was also a Mellor Branch bar between the Windmill and Mellor Brook.

On the Preston Old Road there was the Griffin Gate Turnpike at the bottom of Redlam Brow, and at one time a bar stood at Riley Green, a little further on was the Brindle Lane End bar , and the Hoghton side bar guarded the junction of Finnington Lane with the road from Riley Green.

On the Whalley New Road a toll gate was met with at Brownhill, but on the extension of the borough this was removed to Wilpshire, and remained there until the trust ceased.

On the Darwen road a gate had to be passed through at Ewood, and another, known as the Golden Cup Turnpike, not far from the Anchor Inn.

Toll was taken at Whitebirk, on the Burnley road and bars once stood at the junction of Haslingden Road and Brandy House Brow and also at Shadsworth.

In the Livesey district there were three toll houses: the first was situated at Moorgate Fold, and a mile further on the Livesey Branch Road was the Gib Lane End Turnpike, and after crossing the canal near Feniscowles, dues were exacted from the Livesey Branch Turnpike.

(The original photographs with this article were too poor to recover, and a Burnley artist, Ben Keller, has copied them because of their historical value)

CHAPEL STREET OLD CHAPEL
June 21st 1913

This photograph shows the main entrance in the Chapel Yard which is approached through the gateway at the top of Heaton Street. Its position was under the present organ gallery. In the photograph will be noticed a large window over the door. This was the Tract Room. *(Author's Note: Tract - religious pamphlet)*

Mr. David Campbell was then the secretary of the Tract Department and yesterday while pointing out the position of the old church, he recalled that on the morning of the day of the fire Mr. Walter Briggs, leather merchant, was married in the chapel. The fire originated in the organ loft.

This photograph shows both the church and school on the St. Peter Street side. The tombstones in the foreground are still there. The four windowed building on the left is the school, and the gabled structure on the right the chapel. The low building on the extreme left of the picture is the end of a row of cottages which fronted to Freckleton Street, and which were demolished to make room for the new church. The present spire occupies the site of this end cottage.

An interesting souvenir was published about two months after the fire by Mr. Luke S. Walmsley and has the following information:-

Chapel Street Chapel
Erected 1778
Enlarged 1808
Burned 10th January 1872

CANAL BOATS GROUNDED
October 11th 1913

In common with other East Lancashire towns, Blackburn is suffering from a shortage of water, though this in no way affects the supply in household purposes from the corporation reservoirs. The deficiency is in respect of the Leeds and Liverpool canal, on which traffic has been considerably interfered with. In the centre of the borough this waterway has not been in use since September 14th 1913, a condition of things which has not existed so late in the year for a long period.In fact, the water has been so low between the locks in the Novas district that the canal company have taken advantage of the occasion to effect many repairs to the embankments.

In the photograph men can be seen at work improving the banks, whilst the pebbles in the bed of the canal are clearly discernible. The canal is still used between the boundary of the borough and Nelson, where no locks are situated, but traffic has entirely ceased in other quarters where the locks are in frequent use.

OLD WAREHOUSE IN CLAYTON STREET

December – 1920

When Messrs Birley and Hornby extended their business to Blackburn, and built up the great firm which eventually erected Brookhouse mills, they first had a warehouse in Clayton Street, at that time numbered 25, where they were "Putters Out" to handloom weavers like other merchants of their day.

A warehouse still standing at the top of old Bank Street, in 1920, at a corner behind the Employment Exchange, is pointed out as the one they occupied.

A BIT OF OLD DARWEN STREET
January 19th 1924

There will soon disappear the last of a row of old shops which once stood in Darwen Street and the site of which is now covered, with the exception of the shop referred to, by the Post Office buildings. The present post office was opened in November 1907. Its erection there involved the demolition of the oldest property in Darwen Street. At the other end of the row of shops which stretched from Dandy Walk to the passage leading up to the old Venetian Hall. For over 60 years it was known as the *"Bedding Shop"* and was last in the occupation of Messrs Carlisle as a branch shop of their central premises, the old *"Times"* office buildings in Astley Gate. The lowness of the ceiling, the thickness of the walls and the oak beams indicate the great age of the place.

This end of the row was not as picturesque, perhaps, as the shops at the Dandy Walk end. Many people will remember the quaint shop where for a generation or more Mr. Baines the Fishmonger carried on business, and before that was the saddler's shop of John Myers.

Prior to 1848 the market was held in Darwen Street, which was then perhaps the most important business thoroughfare in the town. One by one bits of property have vanished and the premises been rebuilt, so that the Darwen Street of 1924 has no resemblance to the Darwen Street of old coaching days, when on market days ordinary traffic was conducted with some danger because the stage coaches mainly started and arrived there.

OLD HOUSE IN KING STREET
February 23rd 1924

The house 45 King Street, Blackburn, where Dr. C. M. Bradley now lives, is one of the few residences in that ancient thoroughfare which has not changed in its general appearance with the passing of the years. Soon however, this house will suffer the fate of others in the district, for the corporation have come to an arrangement with the owner, for the removal of the ornamental palisading which obstructs the footpath. This improvement has become all the more necessary since the old vicarage, which stood next door, has been pulled down. There are still buildings in King Street bearing the date 1816, and there is every reason to believe that Dr. Bradley's residence was erected about the same time. It is a large, roomy, substantially built house in the style prevalent in the reign of the Georges.

Two houses are shown in the photograph. The larger one with the fine flight of stone steps leading to the entrance, flanked by massive columns is the residence.

The smaller house, approached by a spiral flight of steps, is used by Dr. Bradley as a surgery.

FLEMING SQUARE

August 23rd 1924

Lying between Darwen Street and Mincing Lane there is an interesting part of Blackburn known as Fleming Square, possessing in at least one instance, architecture that goes back nearly 150 years.

The original Fleming's Square, as it was then known, was erected just a century ago. It was used as a market, possessed a foundry and a cloth hall. The foundry was run by Mr. George Brown, Power Loom and Picker manufacturer. When it was discontinued the premises were converted into a cloth hall.

Originally there were two verandas on the extreme left of Fleming Square, but the bottom one has been converted into business premises, and the roadway through this part is still closed at night by a locked gate. Near the Mincing Lane end there is an ancient staircase in an excellent state of preservation. In some of the cellars under the balcony there are stone pillars that once formed part of the old parish church.

Mr. John Fleming, who was responsible for the erection of the square, was a merchant, born in 1778. He was a trustee for the rebuilding of the parish church in 1819, and having purchased the materials of the old church he used them for building purposes in Fleming Square. Mr. Fleming died in 1842 and his tomb can be found in the parish churchyard.

Down to about 1884 or 1885 the square was patrolled by a night watchman, and twice a year the road was closed for a day (in May and November) by chains drawn across each end, this practice ceasing on the abolition of the toll bars.

TOP FACTORY AT HOGHTON BOTTOMS
August 23rd 1924

Known locally as the top factory because it is situated higher up the River Darwen than its sister mill. The subject of the photograph may be found at Hoghton Valley. It is at the present time somewhat out of date, although not altogether obsolete. It is in direct opposition to the line followed in the erection of present day weaving sheds. The process of weaving cotton goods is carried out on each of the three floors, and until recently all the lighting was obtained from windows in the side of the building. The present management, however, are fully aware of the possibilities of the mill, and are bringing it more up-to-date. To this end they have built a skylight in the roof, and taken portions of the first and second floor's away. This has reduced the number of looms, but the effect has been to come nearer to the modern idea of having as much of the *"top light"* as possible.

The chimney shown is no longer of use, although at one time the low building on the left was occupied by a steam boiler, a large water-wheel is now installed for the purpose of driving the looms, the water being taken by means of the *"cut"* from the River Darwen. Another link with the old days is the bell which calls the work-people to their duties. This bell may be seen under the pigeon loft arrangement on the right of the highest portion of the building.

Photograph: J.H.Taylor, Hoghton.

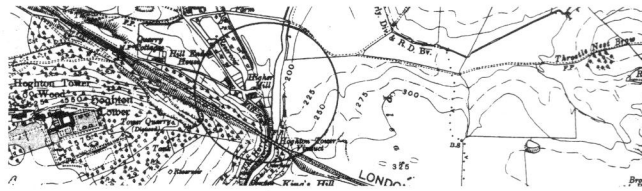

1931 O.S. Map, reproduced by permission of Ordnance Survey

LITTLE HARWOOD HALL
September 13th 1924

Little Harwood Hall is a seventeenth century manor house, built in the usual Elizabethan style on a site near the present St. Stephen's Church. This manor house still retains the two wings, facing south, with flag-slated roofs, and low mullioned windows, no longer lozenge-paned. Unfortunately, the south front, which was the original front, has lately been disfigured, (from the point of view of one who loves old halls), by an extension between the two wings. During the eighteenth century the whole of the north front was rebuilt in brick with plain windows and a central door.

At Little Harwood Hall we find the plain rectangular windows, the Georgian doorway, without portico, but with half columns of stucco, which became very fashionable in the days of the early Georges, and with a fanlight of the real open fan pattern.

In 1815, Thomas Clayton sold Little Harwood Hall with the manor to John Hoyle, of Haslingden, whose son, the late Mr. Henry Hoyle, Solicitor and Clerk to the Magistrates, succeeded to the estate in 1834.

Mr. Hoyle died in 1872 and Little Harwood Hall was sold the following year to Mr. Henry Robinson, of Blackburn. After some years the property was again sold, and it is now used as a club.

SHOP PROPERTY IN DARWEN STREET

December 27th 1924

The photograph shows a bit of old Blackburn. The site, which is in Darwen Street, was situated between St. Peter Street and Mill Lane about the middle of the 19th century. The buildings have now been converted into a number of modern shops and offices, commencing at the headquarters of the Blackburn Philanthropic Mutual Society (formerly the offices of Messrs. Greenwood and Sons, Corn Millers), and Messrs. Stanworth's premises at the junction of Darwen Street and Mill Lane. The vacant space, afterwards used for the construction of the shop occupied by Messrs. Stanworth, formed the entrance to a coal yard kept by the late Mrs. Alice Ainsworth, grandmother of Alderman D. Ainsworth. The building in front of which a young boy is shown standing, was the Old Anchor Inn, kept by Alice Ainsworth, and afterwards tenanted by her son, the Mr. Henry Ainsworth, who subsequently took over the licence of the Wheatsheaf Hotel, then situated on the site of the Philanthropic Mutual Society's offices.

After the Ainsworth family had left the old Anchor Inn, it was taken over by Mr. Hugh Briggs, and on his death his widow, Mrs. Martha Briggs, occupied it until it was demolished and the licences transferred to an hotel in London Road, where she was the first tenant. One of the sons of Mrs. Briggs, the late Mr. James Briggs, kept a Saddler's shop in Darwen Street in those days. Mrs Briggs is shown in the doorway of her hotel.

Alderman Ainsworth still retains the old account book of his grandparents, and this has many quaint and interesting entries. One dated October 3rd 1860, records an amount of 2s-4d owing for rum purchased by *"That woman who comes in with Bob's wife"*. A contract entered into with the late Mr. Hy. Chambers, and dated September 8th 1866, is equally interesting, it reads:-

"I agree to flag the fronts of 12 houses in Lower Audley, and the backyards, for seven pounds".

POET'S CORNER BEERHOUSE
April 4th 1925

William Billington, the poet, at one time kept the Poet's Corner Beerhouse, on Bradshaw Street Blackburn. As will be seen from the photograph it is an unpretentious building standing at the corner of Nab Lane in the centre of Old Blackburn. The property is now amongst the poorest in the town, and the locality has lost proportionately in its character since the days when the Poet's Corner was the haunt of the poet Billington's literary friends.

The Poet's Corner closed its doors as a beerhouse on the night of December 31st 1913. At the licensing sessions of 1912 the renewal of the licence was objected to by the police on the ground of redundancy. Pleading that it has once been occupied by Billington, the poet, and was still in some measure a place of resort by people of literary taste, an effort was made to save the licence.

These sentimental reasons, however, did not carry, and the house was referred for compensation, and, as already mentioned, lost its licence at the end of 1913.

A BIT OF OLD SALFORD

April 18th 1925

The photograph accompanying this article depicts a scene once familiar to older Blackburnians.

It shows part of the old property near to Salford Bridge before the River Blakewater was covered over, and street improvements carried out by the Corporation.

In those days Holme Street was continued from the gable end of the building where Messrs. Townson's confectionery premises are now situated, to the corner of the Bay Horse Hotel, the intervening space, now used as a starting point for the Wilpshire tram cars, being then built upon by the old-fashioned type of house and shop, the erection of which dated back for over a century. Two of the popular shops at that early period were those occupied by the late Mr. Sam Kirtlan, Restaurant Proprietor, and a leading figure in the public life of Blackburn before his death, and by the late Mr. Thos, Kennedy, Oyster Merchant. In the picture will be noticed the once familiar and burly figure of Mr. Kirtlan at the door of his restaurant, which was a popular meeting place for those desirous of discussing the affairs of state, and also those of the corporation. Mr. Kirtlan and his family had resided here for over 40 years, and in those days restaurants were none too plentiful.

Next door are the premises of Mr. Kennedy and his family who occupied them for over 50 years. A little lower down was the old stone bridge over the river which was subsequently set back a considerable distance.

TRAFFIC PROBLEM AT EWOOD
June 13th 1925

The photograph shows work in progress at Ewood, Blackburn, where the iron bridge is being moved back to permit a considerable improvement to this busy thoroughfare. The present width of the roadway is 40 feet, and once the scheme is completed this will be increased to 65 feet, with a footpath extending to 20 feet.

The cost incurred will be £10,800 and an old landmark in the Aqueduct Inn will be taken down, the licence being transferred to a new building at the rear, which is now in the course of erection. Apart from the great convenience which the scheme will afford to vehicular traffic between Blackburn and Darwen, it will be a boon in the football season by assisting to prevent a congestion of people proceeding to and from Ewood Park, a problem which has faced the authorities for many years.

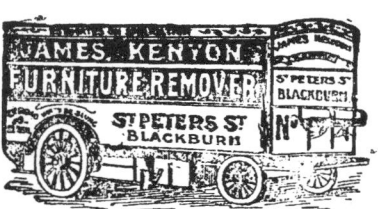

OLD DARWEN STREET
July 25th 1925.

This reproduction of an etching by Mr. J. W. King of Scarboro' depicts a once familiar scene in Darwen Street.

It dates back to the middle of the 19th century, and shows the old property which stood on the site of the present post office. The shop of Mr. Hubert Brooks, the confectioner's store next door, and the newspaper establishment which juts out slightly from the rest, were once familiar landmarks.

Further down the street was the quaint mullion-windowed premises occupied for several years by Messrs. Polding, Corn Millers.

SHORROCK FOLD

August 1st 1925

Shorrock Fold, the much used passage leading from Church Street to Lord Street and the Market Square, is one of the very few parts of central Blackburn unaffected by the march of progress. The secluded house on the right has been used for residential purposes for generations, and it is still so occupied. It was a place of importance before the present Arcade was build by the late Mr. Daniel Thwaites nearly half a century ago. The Church Street site of the Arcade was previously used for residential and business purposes and it was hereabouts that the late Mr. Ellis Nuttall, grandfather of Mr. Ellis Nuttall, M.P. lived for some time, his business premises being situated next door to the Arcade. On the same side there was the shop of the late Mr. Luke Walmsley, Art Dealer, and the premises of Mr. Bradley, a Butcher.

The property in Shorrock Fold has always been exceptionally well kept by its occupants. At one time there were two houses in front of which were fairly large gardens. One house was sacrificed to enable extensions to be made to the rear of the Grosvenor Hotel. It was in Shorrock Fold that two coroners had their headquarters. The late Mr. John Hargreaves was the first to remove here, and he was succeeded by his son, Mr. Henry Unsworth Hargreaves. On the same site was an old licensed house known by the name of the Star Inn. This was demolished when the Arcade was completed.

This photograph looks along Shorrock Fold from Church Street towards Lord Street and the Market Square beyond. The wall just visible on the left of the picture is the rear of the Thwaites Arcade shops. (*At the Lord Street end*

of the Arcade were the toilet facilities for the shops, just 2 'Ladies' and 2 'Gents', it was a regular sight to see staff dashing along the cobbles swing-ing a key on a length of string to let themselves in 'The Loo'. Some shops kept an umbrella by the back door for staff to use when making the dash in the rain. Next to the toilets was a ramp which gave access to the cellars under the arcade. Delivery vehicles would park on Lord Street and large deliveries were loaded on wooden trucks to be wheeled down the ramp then along the long flagged passageway which gave access to the individual cellars of the shops.)

HOG BACK BRIDGE AT SALFORD

August 15th 1925

This sketch by E. Vernon, of Salford Bridge evokes memories of Blackburn long ago. The growing volume of traffic necessitated its removal, and many other improvements have taken place in this busy part of the town. Salford Bridge, which spanned the River Blakewater, used to be the entrance into Old Blackburn from Clitheroe, Burnley and Accrington, the two main roads from East Lancashire converging on it, and meeting originally only a few yards from the bridge itself. Doubtless there was a ford hereabouts in early times for horses and cattle, and possibly stepping stones for foot passengers.

Blackburn takes its name from the River Blakewater, which encircles the main portion of Old Blackburn, from the East round by the South to the West. All the main roads leading into the borough, except Shear Brow and Duke's Brow, had to cross this stream. Formerly, the Salford area consisted of narrow, crooked roads, with old property set at all angles, converging on a humpbacked bridge, but now in place of the bridge there is a big open level space, approached by broad thoroughfares and surrounded by fine buildings.

⚜ ⚜ ⚜

SITE OF THE ARCADE - CHURCH STREET
September 19th 1925

The photograph of the property shown was taken by the late Mr. John Frankland a year or two before it was demolished to provide a site for Thwaites Arcade which was erected in 1883. The high building on the left of the picture is Messrs R. H. & J. Sagars, Watchmakers and Jewellers, who still occupy the premises, The high building on the right of the picture with the white awning is the shop now occupied by Messrs Bowdell Bros, Merchant Tailors, the side of which abuts on Shorrock Lane. At the time the photo was taken it was occupied by Messrs Whittaker, Boot Dealers.

All the property between these two buildings has disappeared, and on the site has arisen Thwaites' Arcade, over which is the Central Conservative Club, and shops occupied by Messrs Lacey's Hosiers and Outfitters, and Messrs Cherry & Sons, Dyers and Cleaners adjoining.

The low building adjoining Messrs Sagar's shop were the premises of Mr. J. Bradley, Butcher, a leading tradesman of his day. The bareheaded gentleman standing in front of the open window is the late Mr. James Sagar, Watchmaker, the lady in white standing next to him is the late Mrs.

Bradley. Her husband was a bit of a character, and the business was managed largely by his wife, who built up a first-class trade. It was a double fronted shop, as can be seen. Mr. & Mrs Bradley lived at the rear of the premises.

Next to the build over passage leading to the rear of the premises was the business establishment of the late Mr. W.H. Cunliffe, Painter and Decorator. The late Mr. Luke S. Walmsley, Art Dealer occupied the shop before Mr. Cunliffe, and at a still earlier period it was occupied by Mr. Henry Briggs, Druggist.

Messrs Dickson and Nuttall's Furnishing Drapers, occupied the remaining block. The shop window was bow fronted, the door being in the centre. Mr. Nuttall, Father of the late Alderman Alfred Nuttall J.P., a former Mayor of Blackburn, and grandfather of Mr. Ellis Nuttall M.P. lived in a house adjoining the shop, and the door of which was reached by a double flight of steps.

Mr. Cunliffe's shop was No. 21 and a large sign at the top informs us that this was the East Lancashire depot for English and French paper-hanging.

OLD PROPERTY IN CHURCH STREET
September 26th 1925

A block of property which stretches from Victoria Street to Holme Street. The shop at the corner of Victoria Street occupied by Hiltons Boot dealers is not shown in the photograph, taken in 1925. Next comes the Golden Lion Inn, then Mr. J. Seller, Fish and Game Dealer, Mr. T. L. Cowburn, Umbrella Manufacturer, Mr. A. Astley, Newsagent and Stationery, and Mr. W. Townson, Sweets Dealer. The next shop is empty, but was formerly occupied by Mr. Walmsley as a commercial hotel and restaurant, then comes the premises of Messrs. F. W. Sutcliffe and Son, Boot Dealers, and the tall building with the spire at the corner of Holme Street, which is also empty, was last tenanted by Messrs. J. Hepworth and Sons Ltd., Clothiers. It has recently been acquired by the Corporation along with other property adjoining in Holme Street, to be used as offices by the Tramways Department. It is hard to realise now that about a century ago residences with palisaded gardens occupied this site of central Blackburn. Though the lower portion of the fronts have undergone alterations out of all recognition, the upper storeys of the lowest buildings in the photograph are the remains of the old residences. Over Mr. Cowburn's shop there is the date 1785 cut in the stone, which to some extent fixes the age of the property.

TELEPHONE: 5913.

TELEGRAMS: "BAGS. BLACKBURN."

THE BLACKBURN PAPER Co Ltd

EMPIRE WORKS.

PLUS ULTRA

PAPER MERCHANTS.
PAPER BAG MAKERS.
GENERAL PRINTERS.
BOOKBINDERS & STATIONERS.

RANDAL STREET, *Blackburn.*

BRIDGE BUILDING AT WHITEBIRK
November 7th 1925

The photo shows the reinforced concrete bridge at Whitebirk in process of construction in connection with the Corporation's Arterial Road scheme. It is expected to be completed in about four month's time, and it will link up an important route from Burnley and East Lancashire generally with Preston, the Fylde, and the West Coast. The Arterial Road will commence at Burnley Road and there will be a straight cut by way of Brownhill, Lammack to Preston New Road. In addition to relieving the congestion in the centre of the Borough, the road is estimated to effect a saving of about two miles to traffic proceeding from Whitebirk to Yew Tree Brow.

The bridge which will span the Leeds and Liverpool canal, is being constructed by Grey's Concrete Co., Glasgow, and will cost a sum of about £7,000. Although not the first reinforced concrete bridge of its kind in the town, it is the initial venture on the Henne-Bique plan.

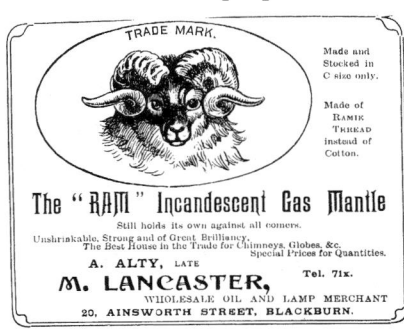

BIRTHPLACE OF W.H.HORNBY
August 20th 1927

The premises 39 King Street, Blackburn were the residence of the Hornby family, whose monogram was in the centre of the iron palisading of the steps leading to the main entrance. W. H. Hornby, Blackburn's first mayor was born here.

When this photograph was taken the premises were occupied by Messrs F. T. Marwood and Co. [Cork Manufacturers, from 1873] and formerly was the home of the Mechanics' Institution, who originated at this residence.

William Henry Hornby was know by old Blackburn politicians as *"Th' Owd Gam Cock"* and as stated above became the First Mayor of Blackburn in 1851.

OLD TOLL HOUSE
January 14ᵗʰ 1928

White Cottage is a picturesque building situated at the junction of four roads. Livesey Branch Road is the main thorough-fare. On the higher part is Gib Lane, and on the lower side Green Lane. The cottage, which is tenanted by Mr. and Mrs Tennant, is reputed to be nearly 200 years old, and it has been owned by the Feilden family, of Witton Park, for a great number of years.

It was once a toll bar and now the surrounding land is rapidly being built upon.

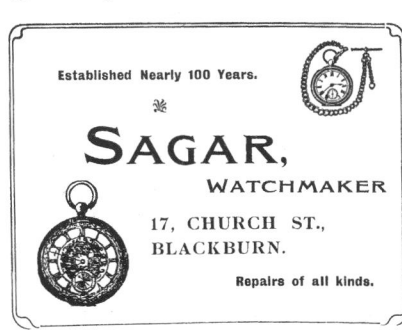

A BIT OF OLD KING STREET
February 11th 1928

The photograph is of some of the oldest property in King Street, where the local gentry mostly resided in the 1820s

Built in 1816, in the reign of George III, two of the houses nearest to old Bank Street, where Cunliffe Brooks laid the foundations of the great banking business now known as Lloyds, are used by the Salvation Army as a hostel for men, and the house next door and part of the fourth house is Mellor's Commercial Hotel. (*This hotel was burned down on March 2nd 1929 with the loss of two lives.*)

ANOTHER TOLL BAR GOING
July 7th 1928

An interesting landmark will shortly disappear in the Whalley New Road district, workmen already having started on the demolition of the old Toll Bar at the junction of Whalley New Road and Whalley Old Road.

By this alteration a blind corner will be removed, as well as a part of history. In the past quite a number of mishaps have occurred at this point, and when the property came onto the market it was purchased by the Corporation for road improvements. It has at this time not yet been decided to what purpose the site will be put. The photograph shows the Toll Bar as it was some years ago.

THUNDER ALLEY CHARITY SCHOOL
July 14th 1928

Of the educational establishments which flourished in Blackburn in the latter half of the 18th Century, not the least interesting was the Girls' Charity School, now in course of demolition to prepare for new shop property. The school, in Thunder Alley, now Town Hall Street, was founded by Mr. William Leyland, who left £200 in trust to establish *"a useful and well ordered charity school for a competent number of poor girls belonging to the town of Blackburn, there to be instructed by a mistress, to be from time to time appointed by said trustees in reading, knitting, sewing and learning the Church Catechism. Also to be there found and provided with books, wool, woollen yarn as the interest and increase of the said sum of £200 will allow."* In the same year £262 subscribed by other well-wishers, was added to the legacy. The school was opened in 1764, a house for the mistress adjoining the premises. The institution prospered, for in 1836 there were 70 scholars in average attendance.

With the passing of the Education Act of 1870, it became clear that the instruction given was not advanced enough for the requirements of the day, and on January 18th of that year the school and the school house in Town Hall Street were sold to the Blackburn Exchange Company, and later the premises were used as auction rooms by Mr. Mark N. Margerison and his son, then by Mr. J.B. Weall and latterly by Messrs. Fletcher, Brown, Son & Co.

The building was of brick, with four windows to the front, with norman tops. Two of the windows contained the original stone mullions to the end.

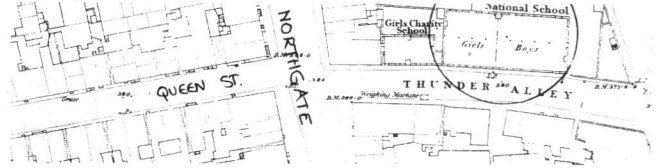

1848 O.S. Map, 60 in to a mile, reproduced by permission of Ordnance Survey

FURTHERGATE CONGREGATIONAL CHURCH
August 18th 1928

The Golden Jubilee of the opening of Furthergate Congregational Church occurs on September 12th. In 1878, on a Thursday afternoon, a large assembly attended the first service, at which the preacher was the Rev. John Hunter of York.

For a long time the Congregationalists of the district had felt the need of a suitable building wherein to worship, and now their aspirations had been realised. The church is an undoubted ornament to the populous suburb of cottages and factories, forming the East End of Blackburn, which is in need of additional architectural features upon which the artistic eye may rest with pleasure.

The history of the cause in the district reveals a determination to succeed that no obstacle could thwart. About 1848 a few members of the James Street Church commenced operations in a disused wheelwright's shop. This was utilised as a Sunday School. So rapidly did the number of scholars increase that it soon became apparent that fresh quarters would have to be found. Accordingly, a plot of land at the corner of Harwood Street was purchased. On this site a school was erected and opened in 1851. As a requisition by members of the congregation at Furthergate to the church at James Street. To be allowed to establish a separate church was granted in 1874. The foundation stone was laid in September 1877, and a year later the church opened. The architecture is gothic, the external walls being of Darwen parpoints, with dressings of Longridge stone. The total accommodation is for nearly 800 persons. The cost approximated £5,000 and including a grant of £500 from the Lancashire Congregational Chapel Building Society.

FARMHOUSE WITH A CURIOUS NAME

October 6th 1928

The photograph shows White Barn Door Farm, belonging to the estate of Mr. Robert Peel of Knowlmere Manor, which is to be demolished by Blackburn Corporation to complete the new arterial road from Intack to Preston New Road, a thoroughfare extending over four and a half miles. The farm is at present occupied by Mr. Thomas Haworth, farmer, and previous tenants were Mr. Mytton and Mr. Reeday. Mr. John Walker, was the occupier for over 20 years and his son Mr. H. Walker, wheelwright, of Whitebirk Road, said he could not explain how it was the house came to have such a strange title. There is an interesting stone embedded in the house wall which reads:- "**B.E.G.E. 1768**". Exactly what this signifies no-one appears to know.

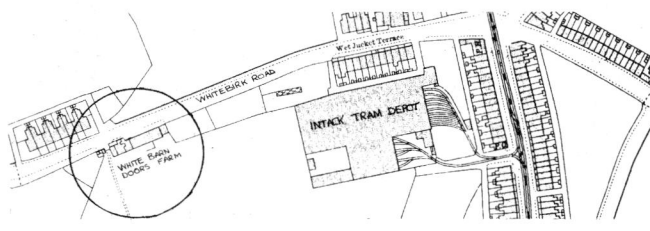

1911 O.S. Map, 25 inches to a mile, reproduced by permission of Ordnance Survey

ST. PAUL'S FOUNDRY DEMOLISHED
October 20th 1928

An old and historic building formerly known as St. Paul's Foundry, but more popularly designated *"Railton's Forge"*, St. Paul's Avenue, has just been demolished. It is impossible to state the origin of the premises with any degree of certainty, but in the early years of last century it was in full use as a foundry and was occupied by Robert Railton, Senior. Presumably the business flourished and the premises were extended, for in the Rate Book of 1845 reference is made to a new foundry occupied by Robert Railton together with workshop, foundry, weighing machine, stable, office, warehouse, etc., adjoining.

In 1830 the names of Robert and John Railton were bracketed with that of their father, and the two brothers were shown to occupy a house in Nab Lane, in close proximity to the works. The foundry was acquired many years ago by the Corporation, the site being reserved for an extension of the technical college. For several years it has been used as a store, thought at one time it served the purpose of a typography class in connection with the technical college. Access to the top storey was by an outside flight of wooden steps, as seen in the photograph. A portion of the new foundry is still used by the Corporation for storage purposes. A descendant of the Railton family was the Rev. Robert Railton, who started life as a Compositor at the "Blackburn Times" printing works. He eventually took holy orders, became curate at St. Barnabas Church, married the daughter of Mr. Isaac Ward of Bank Villas, and was for many years rector of St. James' Church, Clitheroe.

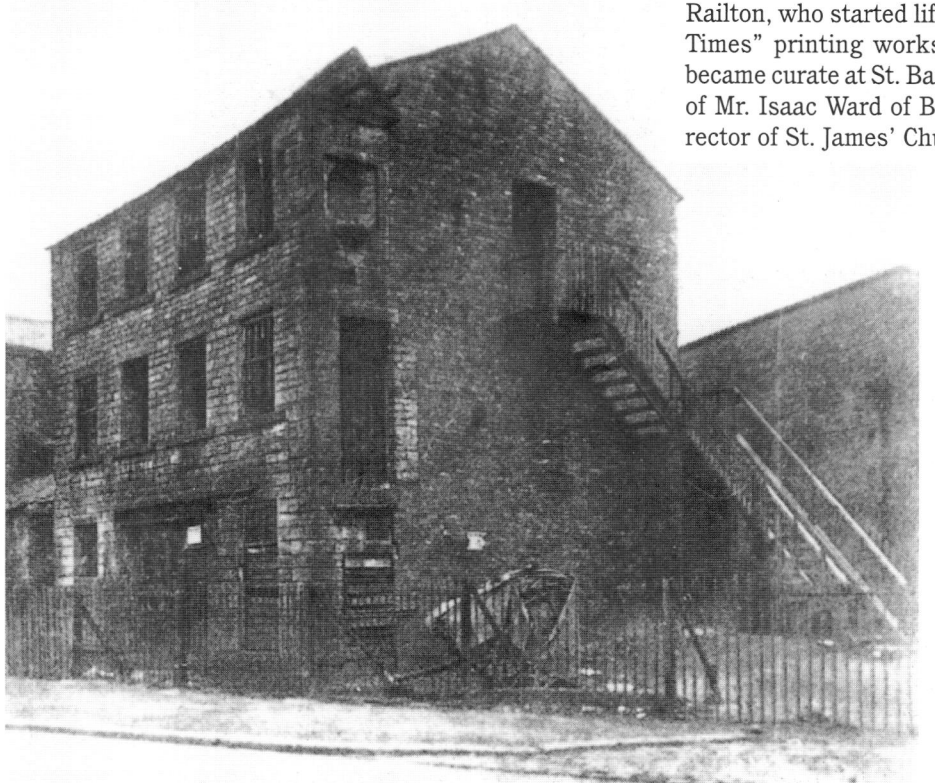

PICTURESQUE DOME TO BE RETAINED

December 15th 1928

The last remaining portion of the Co-operative Society's old premises in Northgate is now in the course of demolition, and before many days have passed it will be a thing of the past. The attractive landmark at the junction of Northgate and Town Hall Street, in the form of a stone dome and flag staff, is to be retained and placed on the new building as an interesting link with the old headquarters, and also because of its outstanding characteristics.

The Amalgamated Cco-operative Society opened their Central Stores in Northgate and Town Hall Street in March 1905, the official ceremony being performed by Mr. James Sharples, President for several years.

The fine premises now being erected occupy a site on which formerly stood the Mason's Arms; at the corner, a butchers shop, conducted for several years by the late Alderman Garsden. Tthe office of the Great Northern Railway Company, the shop of Mr. Parker, painter and decorator, and lastly the Central Warehouse and Offices of Messrs. Hart and Son, rope and twine manufacturers. On the Northgate Side of the Mason's Arms was the establishment of Messrs. Shaw and Porter, Saddlers, and the Auction Room and Furniture Emporium of Messrs. Ratcliffe, the head of which subsequently settled in Canada. Incidentally part of the site was once utilised by an old Blackburn character, Mr. Mercer, who had his smithy there. (*see opposite*)

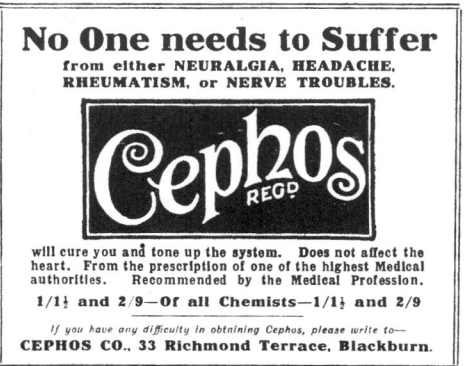

SMITHY ON NORTHGATE

January 5th 1929

The old Smithy in Northgate, which occupied part of the site utilised by theCo-operative Society. The smithy, which was immediately facing The Jolly Sailor pub was taken over about 1869 by Mr. John Spencer (seen on the left of photo) who died about 1909 at the age of 79. It is believed that the smithy was in existence for close upon a century, and it is a reminder of the days when horses furnished the motive for transport. The smithy was later transferred to Queen Street, where it was subsequently pulled down when the Blakey Moor alterations commenced prior to 1929. The business was carried on in St. Paul's Avenue by Mr. John Spencer (Jnr) (third from the left). Mr. John Troughton (second from left) lived in Snig Brook. In the vicinity of the smithy when it stood in Northgate were the Mason's Arms, Messrs Shaw and Porter, saddlers, Mr. John Brewer, chemist, and the Mason's Arms Yard.

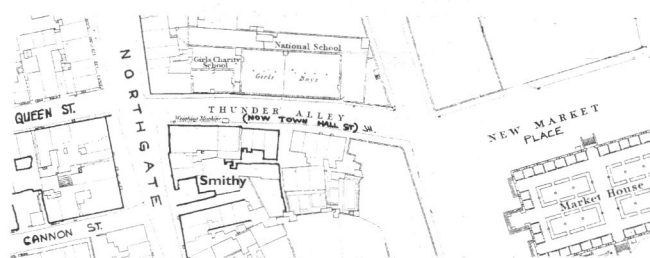

1848 O.S. Map, 60 inches to a mile, reproduced by permission of Ordnance Survey

DUKE STREET MILL
March 2ⁿᵈ 1929

The acquisition of Duke Street mill by the Blackburn Corporation will probably mark the end of its career as a centre for the manufacture of Dhootie Cloths for the Indian market.

Containing 471 dobby looms and employing 180 operatives, the shed was closed down in March 1928, and it is expected that the site will be utilised for the purpose of central improvements. Messrs Arthur Shutt & Co. were the last firm to occupy the mill. Previously it was run by Messrs.

William & Richard Greenwood. In the outer wall of the preparation department, overlooking the yard and close to the chimney stack, is a stone inscription bearing the initial "J.A." and the date 1834. The initials refer to Mr. John Ainsworth. The site is regarded as one of great antiquity. In the basement are evidences that at one time hand-looms were accommodated here. Succeeding owners have enlarged the building from time to time.

IN THE DAYS OF THE STAGECOACH
April 20th 1929

The photo shows an old and familiar part of Blackburn, dating back to the early days of the last century, when the stage coach ran between Manchester, Blackburn and Preston. It was at this spot in Canterbury Street that there was a change of horses, and although the premises have been in the occupation of the late Mr. Henry Aspin and his son, as a forge and smithy for something like a score of years the stables are still in excellent state of preservation. The walls are something like a yard in thickness and the whole premises have a very solid appearance. In the photograph can be seen the well worn stone steps by which the gentry of bygone days used to mount their horses, the property is owned by Messrs. Daniel Thwaites and Co. Brewers.

♣   ♣   ♣

DANDY WALK SMITHY

June 29th 1929

The illustration of the Old Smithy on Dandy Walk, is from a pen and ink sketch by Mr. Harry S. Fairhurst, made in 1891.

Joseph Harrison came to Blackburn from Ingleton about the year 1829, and worked at his trade as a blacksmith in Dandy Walk. He soon became a machine-maker, and in the middle of the 19th century (1851-52) he held all the patents of Messrs. Hornby, Keirworthy and Bullough, for warping, sizing and weaving machinery, and at the Crystal Palace exhibition in Hyde Park, 1851, Joseph Harrison and Sons were appointed machinists to H.R.H. The Prince Consort. In 1854 Henry Harrison, then a youth of 17, had charge of his father's great exhibit, and afterwards until his marriage he was continental traveller for Bank Foundry.

The Dandy Walk is at present just a short cut to the railway station, and before the Palace Theatre was built, it ended in a footbridge, leading to the station. When the railway station was first built, people using Dandy Walk had to turn sharp left along a footpath by the Riverside, between river and churchyard, until a footbridge was reached nearly at the bottom of Station Road now Railway Road and then on up the path to Spring Gardens and High Street. The river was covered over when the boulevard was constructed in 1886.

❖ ❖ ❖

THUNDER ALLEY
July 27th 1929

The corner of Northgate and Town Hall Street, is the only bit left of that interesting old thoroughfare, Thunder Alley. The cottage which the alert policeman seems to be guarding, though he is only posing for the photographer in, has a doorway so low that he would have to stoop a lot if he wanted to get inside. Yet it is a landmark in Blackburn history, for in the first half of the 19th century, this cottage was occupied as a barber's shop by the father of an old townsman Henry Ward and in this shop he used to shave Daniel Thwaites for a halfpenny.

Next door to the Barber's on the right of the photograph is seen the cottage occupied for a hundred years or more by successive mistresses of the Girls' Charity School, founded in 1764. From a legacy of £200 from the will of William Leyland of King Street. Town Hall Street was then called *Thunder Alley*, and was an important thoroughfare across Northgate until the modern public halls and sessions house were built. Thunder Alley continued, almost in a direct line, to Blakey Moor, under the name of Queen Street, the most important of the old streets on the west side of Northgate.

UNION STREET BRIDGE
August 24th 1929

At the beginning of the 19th Century St. John's district was growing rapidly, and was in favour as a residential district for the lesser gentry who did not aspire to live in King Street, and for the Calico Manufacturers who had mills and warehouses on the riverside between Salford Bridge and Union Street Bridge. It was early marked out as a town build site by the Stone Bridges over the Blakewater, in Union Street and Salford, leading in from the main roads on the East. When St. John's Church was erected in 1788 it became a fashionable quarter.

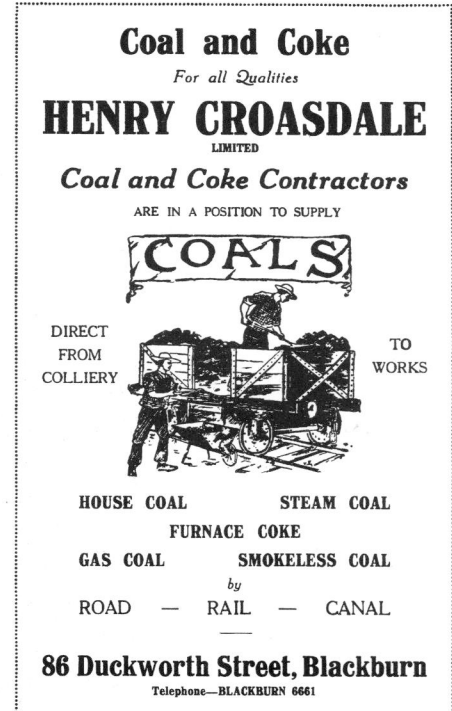

ALL HALLOWS WELL
August 31st 1929

In bygone days water came from three wells in Blackburn. All Hallows Well was nearest the Parish Church, and more distant were Folly Well and Brookhouse Well. They were all close to the Blakewater and it is said that their waters were cool and clear.

All Hallows Well - a holy well in earlier days associated maybe with one of the first Christian missionaries, in the 17th Century, and was visited by folk from outside the town who carried away the water to treat bad eyes. There is a spring near the Wellington Inn, Livesey, which was said to have had the same healing virtues.

The All Hallows Well is situated in the area behind the Adelphi Hotel.

CANAL MILL, EANAM
September 7th 1929

The first steam powered corn mill of Blackburn and the oldest cotton mill on the canal now standing, is the small stone built spinning and weaving shed close to Navigation Bridge, built by George Clark.

It is now known as Canal Mill, and at present is vacant. It was last used as a storehouse in connection with Yates's foundry. The photograph is taken from the canal bank and the building appears on Gillies' map of 1822. The mill eventually became Higher Eanam Brewery.

Begun in 1770, the Leeds and Liverpool canal took 46 years to complete, and construction was begun at both ends. In 1810 the offices of the canal company were established at Eanam (Navigation Bridge). The canal finished at Nova Scotia in 1816, and was in that year opened through from Leeds to Liverpool. In Blackburn the company soon began to reap the reward of their labours by selling land to the builders of mills and obtaining traffic from the mills as soon as they were built.

THE OLD CALENDAR HOUSE
September 14th 1929

Between Union Street and Penny Street there is a short street knows as Old Chapel Street, in which may be seen the building with round-headed windows (originally filled with coloured glass) depicted in our photograph of the *Old Calendar House*.

It was known as the Old Calendar House because it was originally the Machine Shop of a local manufacturer and had been used as such before being purchased and adapted as a place of worship for the Methodist Society formed in the town about the year 1780. John Wesley preached in Blackburn in 1780 and again in 1781. It is at present the warehouse of a marine store dealer, whose deeds record that it was formerly a Wesleyan Chapel.

OLD COTTAGES TO DISAPPEAR

October 5th 1929

Three picturesque, ivy-covered cottages, which for generations have formed a landmark at the junction of Preston New Road and Revidge Road, will soon be a thing of the past. The work of demolition commenced a few days ago and the land, when cleared, will be added to the garden space of Mr. John Edmondson, of Arlgy, who has had an option on the property for several years. A farmhouse stood on the site in the early days, and when the land was taken over for building purposes the farm buildings were converted into three cottages. The property belonged to the Troy estate, and in the lifetime of Mrs. Thwaites the tenancies were not disturbed. There was hope at one period that the Ccorporation would acquire a portion of the land to round off the bend at this busy crossroads, but this has not come to fruition.

BROOKHOUSE MILLS
December 28th 1929

The illustration shows two large blocks called the New Mills, then the weaving shed, on the site of the old hand loom cottages, and the small spinning mill of 1828. On the right is seen the old mill, dated 1832. There are really two old mills, but in the perspective of the drawing they blend into one. The one dated 1832 is six storeys high, including the basement, and nine windows long. It is substantially built of stone, but up the side of the staircase tower there has been built a more modern addition in brick to provide for the necessary hoist.

About 1809, Messrs Birley and Hornby bought Derrikan's field at Brookhouse and built a size house there. Two buildings are shown in Gillies' map. One of them was Birley and Hornby's size-house and the other a bleaching-house used by the Peels. According to tradition it was adjoining these two small buildings that Birley and Hornby erected their first spinning mill, in 1828. It was run by water power. The small spinning mill can be seen in the centre of our illustration, with a large weaving shed now adjoining it. Four years after the small spinning mill was built there was a much larger one put up.

CICELY HOLE FARM
March 15th 1930

Near Cicely Bridge there was an old farmhouse called Cicely Hole. It was on a high bank belonging to the Railway Company, and a remnant of it is still in existance. Some part of this building may be hundreds of years old, but the front door has been masked by the modern lean-to shed shown in the foreground of our photograph. The old Cicely Hole Farm is a bit of old Blackburn that has been pushed very much into the background by the march of town planning. Its awkward situation on a high bank of the railway accounts for this. The farm was originally 6 acres in extent and was part of the vicarial glebe before the building of the railway station.

ROPE SHOP ON CHURCH STREET

June 21st 1930

Thomas Hart, the founder of an old Blackburn business which has continued and prospered down to the present day, was born at Leyland about the year 1750.

In 1789 he is said to have come to Blackburn and commenced business as a roper in the fields beyond the Blakewater, a little to the east of St. John's Church, then in the course of erection.

Thomas married Martha Almond and they had three children, Bridget, William and Thomas. All were infants when he died in 1802. Mrs Hart, the widow, must have been a capable woman; she carried on the business during the minority of her children, give her sons a good education, and brought them up in the fear and love of God. The name of Martha Hart appears in the earliest directory of Blackburn, published by Thomas Rogerson in 1818, in which she is described as Martha Hart, Rope Manufacturer, carrying on business in Church Street. This house and shop existed unaltered until 1874 and is the subject in our photograph. The Golden Lion Hotel is shown next door, occupied by John Fisher. Mrs Hart held the premises on a yearly lease from Henry Sudell. They stood on a site of 207 square yards at the corner of Church Street and Ainsworth Street, for at that time Victoria Street had not been constructed, and Ainsworth Street began at the New Inn. In 1859 the corporation decided to widen Ainsworth Street at its junction with Church Street, and open Victoria Street into Church Street. Twelve years later they purchased a strip of land for the purpose from Messrs. Hart, along the Ainsworth Street frontage of their shop and constructed a footpath 7ft wide, besides slightly widening the roadway. Victoria Street had already been cut through to Church Street, and the new footpath at Hart's corner at once became one of the busiest thoroughfares in the town.

DICKINSON'S FOUNDRY

July 5th 1930

Dickinson's Foundry was established in King Street, near King Street Bridge, in the year 1826. Its object was to produce power looms to supersede the hand looms of Blackburn weavers, who were totally unable to cope with the world-wide demand that had sprung up for cotton goods, or to use up the cotton yarn produced on Arkwright's and Crompton's new spinning machines. The founder was William Dickinson. William Thorp, the builder of King Street Mill was his uncle, and before Mr. Dickinson set up business as an ironfounder and machinist in partnership with his uncle, he experimented with the machinery at King Street mill.

Messrs. Dickinson and Thorp's premises later formed part of the extensive cotton mills of Feilden, Thorp. and Townley, Harley Street mills, and William Dickinson, who was shortly left to carry on the machine making business alone, called his works "*Phoenix Foundry*", though it appears in the directory of 1852 as "*Harley Street Foundry*".

The artist's drawing belongs to the owners of Dickinson's Foundry, and shows the entrance to the courtyard of King Street Mill, with Dickinson's furnace close behind the arched gateway. But Harley Street Foundry (named Phoenix Foundry in the ordnance survey of 1844), was the place where he began to make the Blackburn loom on a large scale. Harley Street, off Leyland Street, now a cul de sac with only 3 houses in it, was originally a long street of cottages leading to a footbridge over the Blakewater, and thence on to Pump Street. Phoenix Foundry was behind the cottages, on the riverside, opposite Whalley Banks Mill.

At the time of his death on the 19th of June 1882, his residence was Cambay Villas, Preston New Road. He was 77 years of age. For many years he had given up active participation in business.

His tomb is in the Church of England portion of Blackburn Cemetery, immediately opposite the church.

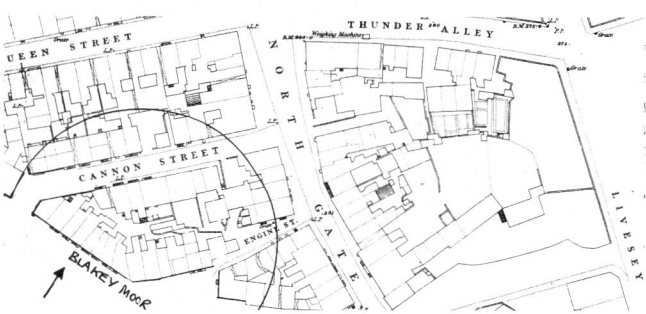

OLD BLAKEY MOOR

December 27th 1930

The sketch drawn by Harry S. Fairhurst in 1891 shows a view of old property on Blakey Moor between Queen Street and Engine Street, which faced the new Technical College. In those days Old Northgate followed much the same line as the present thoroughfare, except that it continued without a break to Limbrick.

Engine Street was a short cut from the top of Blakey Moor and Northgate and once housed the Blackburn fire engine in a brick building on that street. The area shown in the sketch is now the site of the present public halls.

1894 O.S. map, 25 inches to a mile, by permission of the Ordnance Survey.

MILL HILL CLOCK
February 8ᵗʰ 1931

An interesting ceremony was performed at Mill Hill on Saturday, when the fine public clock and Cambridge Chimes, constructed in the new tower of the Congregational Church, were formally started by Mr. T. Greenwood, the chief promoter of the venture. The total cost is £250, and of this amount Mr. Greenwood has succeeded in raising £200 from persons belonging to all religious denominations.

Alderman E. Hamer, J.P. presided, and there were also present the Revs J. P. Wilson, T. J. Barker, W. J. Parson, J. W. Rose and Mr. Allen (Coventry), Mr. H. W. Ellison, Mrs T. Greenwood, Councillor E. Hamer, Mr. J. W. Atkinson, and Mr. J. T. Henshaw M.S.A. (the Architect) of Blackburn and Burnley.

Alderman Hamer having apologised for the absence of the mayor, said their handsome clock and its chimes would, he had no doubt, give some excellent lessons to people all round. It would also be a good reminder to those who attended places of worship in the district on Sunday. After more speeches, Mr. T. Greenwood then set the clock in motion with a rope which had been fixed to the communion rail, and attached to the clock's works. Two years ago the church had got into such a dilapidated state that it became imperative that they should restore it, and the committee came to the conclusion that the only way this could be satisfactorily done was by erecting a new exterior wall. In the midst of the discussion - and the scheme involved a cost of £1,200 - the wind was taken out of them by a suggestion on the part of Mr. Greenwood that provision would be made for the clock. His enquiries showed that £250 would be required to put his proposal into operation, and he gave the assurance that the money would be forthcoming.

EARLY BANKING IN BLACKBURN

February 21st 1931

THE BLACKBURN BANK FOR SAVINGS 1818

Blackburn was a rapidly growing town when the Government originally sent forth its call to the workers to invest their small savings in the National Debt, and in 1818 (within a year of the passing of the first Act) a *"Bank for Savings"* was established in this town. It existed only for eleven or twelve years, and possibly came to an unsatisfactory end, but information is very meagre.

A committee of local gentlemen obtained a copy of the Act of Parliament (Act 57, George III, Cap 130) and drafted a scheme which was submitted to a public meeting held in the grammar school, in the old churchyard, under the presidency of the Rev. Thomas Starkie, Vicar, on Friday February 9th 1818, at 12 o'clock. *"At which meeting all the ground rules previously prepared at another meeting be adopted, and a subscription list be entered into, and the lists be left at different newsrooms. That the fund to be raised be called the auxiliary fund, and be at the disposal of the committee of managers."*

The first *Agent* of the bank, who combined the duties of actuary, cashier and clerk, was Joseph Messenger, who was appointed at a meeting of the committee of managers, held at the Grammar School on February 23rd 1818. He held office until his death in 1821.

The bank was held in a room in France Street, off King Street, once a week, for two hours only, and was opened for the first time on Saturday afternoon, March 7th 1818. The deposits on the first day amounted to £124. The agent lived in the centre of the town and in 1820, the bank was removed to his house in the square. The end of this first Blackburn bank for savings is somewhat obscure, but the depositors appear to have been paid off about the middle of 1829.

NURSERYMEN
SEEDSMEN
SCOTCH GROWN SEED POTATOES
MANGEL, CLOVER, and GRASS
WILD FLOWER and BIRD
WE SAVE YOU MONEY

ELECTRICITY
BANISHES
SMOKE·
FUMES
& DIRT

FOR LIGHT, HEAT & POWER
IN HOME, OR WORKSHOP.
Full particulars of Blackburns Electrical Advantages
from The Chief Electrical Engineer,
Corporation Electricity Department,
Jubilee Street   Blackburn. *Phone No 4211.*

THE OLD MUSIC HALL
April 4ᵗʰ 1931

The Music Hall in Market Street Lane (corner of Mincing Lane) is still standing, and it was used for all kinds of purposes, including a circus, and was the home of the Mechanics' Institute and the Philosophical Society. In 1831 it opened its doors to the inauguration of the Temperance Society.

Originally called the "*Old Assembly Rooms*" and built in 1787, it was converted to "*The Music Hall*" and later "*Papa Page's Lyceum Theatre*" in 1851.

BIT OF OLD BLACKBURN

May 2ⁿᵈ 1931

A picturesque corner in the centre of town, this bit of old Blackburn stands at the corner of Kirkham Lane and Limbrick and forms part of a block of buildings which has been the subject of many a photographer.

The newsagent's shop a little lower down in Limbrick has the date 1765 carved on the lintel over the doorway.

♣　　♣　　♣

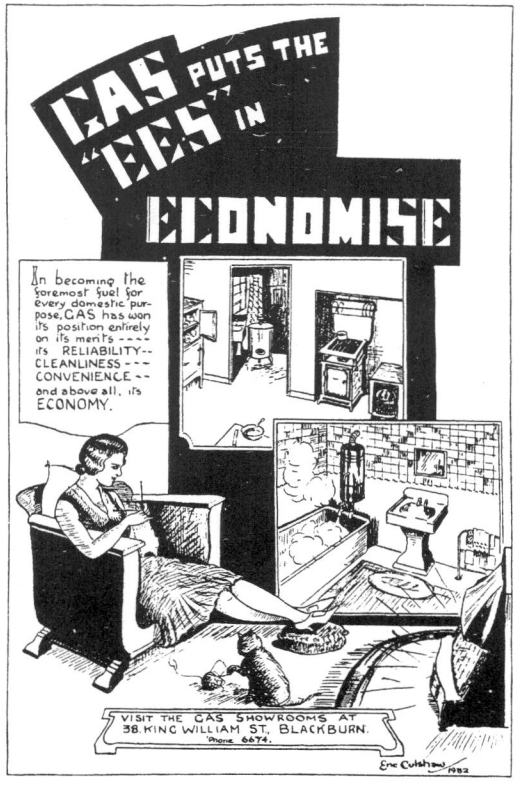

GAS PUTS THE "EES" IN ECONOMISE

In becoming the foremost fuel for every domestic purpose, GAS has won it's position entirely on it's merits ---- it's RELIABILITY-- CLEANLINESS --- CONVENIENCE -- and above all, it's ECONOMY.

VISIT THE GAS SHOWROOMS AT 38, KING WILLIAM ST, BLACKBURN. Phone 6674.

Eric Culshaw 1982

BLACKBURN EXCELSIOR CO-OP
May 9th 1931

Next year the Society reaches its Diamond Jubilee and the management invite those imbued with the co-operative spirit to swell the ranks and try to make 1932 a record year. They welcome any enquiries and comparisons, whether your requirements are provisions, drapery, furniture, footwear, coal, or indeed, anything for the household.

The movement had its inception at a small store in Addington Street some 59 years ago, a photograph of which is the topic of this article. The resolution to form the society being approved at a meeting of associates on December 3rd, 1872, it became registered on March 8th the following year.

A visit to the store in Lambeth Street will convince anyone that they can maintain their obligations to over 700 members, and still sell their commodities at competitive prices. Anyone can enrol by payment of an entrance fee of one shilling.

WENSLEY FOLD MILLS
June 13th 1931

William Eccles, having prospered in his profession as an attorney, decided to enter the cotton trade, and to enter it in a big way.

Robert Hopwood Senior, had given a lead by the building of Nova Scotia Mill ("*Hopput's Factory*"). On an adjacent plot of land, William Eccles built Commercial Mills ("*T' Brick Factory*"), and became one of the half dozen great employers of the town. From the first Mr. Eccles showed every consideration for his work- people. On a plot of ground he had acquired on the opposite side of Sawmill Lane, reserved as a site for an additional weaving shed, he set out 60 or 70 garden plots and allotted them to such of his work-people as had a taste for cottage gardening, and were glad of the change to grow their own vegetables.

From Nova Scotia, after he had prospered in the trade, Mr. Eccles extended his enterprise to Wensley Fold by the purchase of Wensley Fold Mill. The old mill, of which very little trace now remains, was the first cotton mill in Blackburn, the second being Spring Hill Mill, built in 1797. In 1824, by which time the number of spinning mills had increased to eight, Wensley Fold, rebuilt, was run by Messrs. T and R. Lund and J. Foster, and it was this old mill that William Eccles bought in the 1840s. Mr. Eccles built a large new mill, adjacent to the old one, the easterly block of the Wensley Fold mills now existing, and prepared to extend his business still further, though at that time he was already employing 1,350 workers. Mr. Eccles provided additional cottages for his work hands at Wensley Fold, and showed himself in esteem by providing them with some public baths. The new mill was up-to-date in every way. It had a weaving shed 70 yards long by 100 yards broad.

The photograph shows Wensley Fold mills in 1931. The old mill was on the site of Messrs. Birtwistle Fielding's weaving shed, seen on the left of the picture. It was pulled down sixty years ago. The new mill built by Mr. Eccles in 1852 is the large mill on the right of the photo and is now standing empty.

CLAYTON STREET WESLEYAN CHURCH
January 9th 1932

The Golden Jubilee of the present Wesleyan Church in Clayton Street is to be celebrated with special gatherings, commencing with a reunion of past and present scholars next Saturday, while next Sunday the pulpit will be occupied by the Rev. J. T. Wardle Stafford, who will lecture on the Monday. The celebrations will conclude on March 23rd with a visit from the Conference President.

The present building shown in the photograph, is the third chapel erected at Clayton Street, which for about a century and a half has been the head of the Blackburn circuit, and a pillar of Methodism in the town. The first chapel, completed in the year 1786, was opened by John Wesley. It remained until 1815, when it was rebuilt. The second chapel served for 65 years, and then the present building took its place. It was opened with special services on January 15th, 22nd and 29th, in 1882.

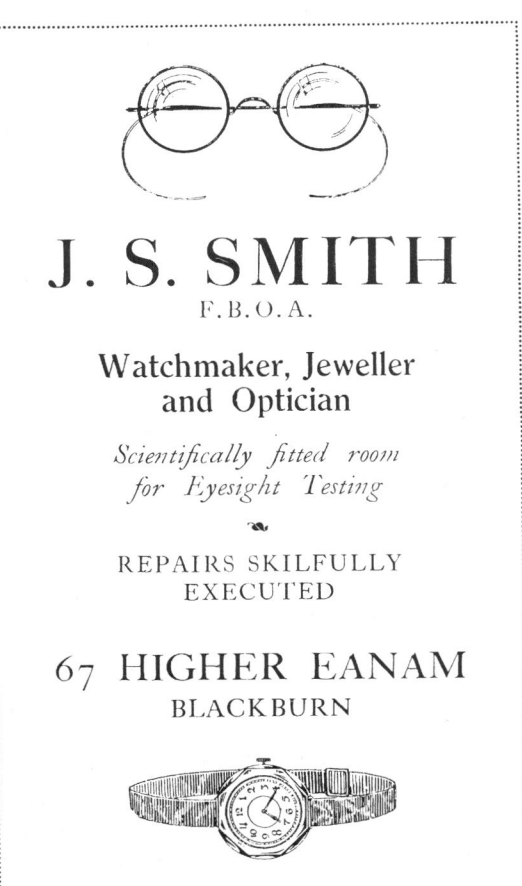

ROMAN ROAD UNEARTHED
January 16th 1932

The sketch is a view of the Roman Road unearthed within the borough of Blackburn at Blackamoor. It is engraved from a photograph taken by Mr. R. P. Gregson, and is of the paved road discovered 4ft-6in below the road in the centre of the little hamlet. Apparently the whole population of the neighbourhood have been attracted by the discovery, and hundreds of townsmen have walked up to see it. The crossroad is one leading from Feniscowles through Lower Darwen to Guide and Oswaldtwistle. In 1890, while laying a main sewer along Stopes Brow, Lower Darwen, the Blackburn Corporation workmen had to cross the old Manchester-To-Ribchester Roman Road at Blackamoor, and at this crossing, at a depth of 4ft-6in, below the modern surface, they came across a rude stone pavement and reported the fact to the Borough Engineer, Mr.

McCallum, who recognised it as the actual road made by the Roman legions,

Mr. McCallum then ordered his men to leave the road undisturbed and tunnel a passage underneath it for the main sewer, so the road is still there just as he found it. The surface is seen to consist of irregular blocks of stone, arranged as "*setts*", and beneath these there is a substratum of gravel, two feet six inches in thickness, made solid by pressure and looking very much like a nineteenth century macadam road. The surrounding and underlying natural ground is of clay. The length of the trench in the illustration is eight feet, and this shows eight feet of the width of the Roman Road, which runs in the direction indicated by the street sign. The sewer was being laid at right angles to it. This is by far the most interesting section of the Roman road ever laid bare by modern excavations within the borough of Blackburn.

MEMORIAL FOUNTAIN-DARWEN STREET

February 6th 1932

Under the railway bridge at the entrance to Park Road there is a drinking fountain bearing the following inscription *"1858 Erected by the Friends of the late George Dewhurst"*. George was a reedmaker in Queen Street more than a hundred years ago.

His name appears in the directory of 1824, but not in that of 1818, and it appears again, 34 Queen Street, in 1851.

It was as a demagogue, perhaps a little ahead of his time, that George sprang into fame, for, in his early days, he was imprisoned for two years in Lancaster Castle for sedition. His offence was *"opening his mouth too wide"* before the days of free speech. On his return home from Lancaster Castle he became a popular leader in social and municipal affairs as well as in politics. Blackburn's desire to benefit under the Reform Bill had the effect of drawing all parties together when the bill was before parliament, and in the year 1831 the local *"Political Union"* comprising men of all parties, held weekly meetings. Mr. William Feilden (afterwards Sir William) a Whig, was the leader of the movement, and Dewhurst, the Radical, no longer counted a revolutionist but a patriot, was cheered when the was seen walking in procession, arm-in-arm with Mr. Feilden, to a town's meeting on Blakey Moor called to petition parliament in support of Lord John Russell's second Reform Bill.

Perhaps it was the strength of Liberalism under the Pilkington leadership that caused this memorial to the old radical to be placed in Park Road under Darwen Street railway bridge. Park Road School at that time was a great centre of liberal propaganda, and round Christ Church School there was a hotbed of Toryism. Durham stated that the measures of reform for advocating which George Dewhurst suffered for two years imprisonment, though then deemed seditious, were nothing like so sweeping or so extensive as those afterwards advocated by the conservative members of the borough.

GRIMSHAW PARK POTTERY

February 6th 1932

When Charles Haworth made this drawing for "*Bits of Old Blackburn*" in 1889, the landmark it depicts had completely disappeared. It stood in a "*Potters Field*" on "*Pottery Hill*" in "*Pottery Lane*" (Haslingden Road) and many people around 1882 possessed washing mugs, bread mugs, big brown cooking dishes, and flower pots that had been baked in the oven in the illustration. But pottery as an industry never became established in Blackburn. The local clay was only suitable for the coarsest brownware, and, after the closing of the pottery, Blackburn productions in clay were limited to drain pipes and bricks.

Grimshaw Park makes these to this day, as it made them in 1824, and even at that date brick had begun to compete with stone as a local building material.

The oven is marked on Gillies' map. It stood on the line of Roman Road, in Haslingden Road, close to the South West corner of the grounds of the present work house, but it had originated in an earlier pottery in Kemp Street, owned by Messrs. Kemp and Riley. That was a thatched building, which was burnt down early in the nineteenth century.

Mr. Thomas Kemp then retired from business, but his partner, Mr. Riley built the new pothouse in Haslingden Road and carried on. The ordnance map of 1848 shows this exactly as it has been shown by Gillies, but names it "*Old Pottery*", which suggests that it had then fallen into disuse. Local residents in 1889, said that it had been standing empty for forty, or perhaps fifty, years.

HOLE I' TH' WALL HOTEL

February 13th 1932.

No part of the borough is undergoing change more rapidly than the Shear Brow and Four Lanes End district, and it is quite possible that if the present rate of progress of building is maintained, in a few years from now most of the old property still remaining will have disappeared.

On the left hand side of Shear Brow, going up from Limbrick, a little beyond the end of East Park Road, and almost exactly opposite the Hole-I'-Th'-Wall Hotel, is a little low, old stone building with a porch. It is not generally known that this is the old Hole-I'-Th'-Wall Hotel. In the absence of any records it is impossible to fix the period at which it was built, but that it is of a great age. The walls are 18 inches to two feet thick, and the porch, with its seat of stone, is another indication of its great age. Mr. John Fletcher, of Shear Brow,

informs us that his grandmother Mrs. Hayhurst, who died about 1902 at the great age of 82, and who was born and lived in the locality all her life, used often to speak of her early recollections. When she was a girl Shear Brow was an important highway, and the old Hole-I'-Th'-Wall was a well known house of call. Mrs Hayhurst's father kept a team of pack-donkeys at Lanes End. These donkeys were used for carrying sand in their panniers from Stonyhurst to Darwen and Tockholes, and taking back coals. At the end of a day's journey Old Hayhurst often stopped at the old Hole-I'-Th'-Wall for a "*camp*", leaving the donkeys on the highway, where they could be seen from the Lanes End by his wife, who used to send her daughter, the Mrs. Hayhurst recently deceased, to bring them home. In those days seats were placed at the front of the hotel, where men sat smoking their Churchwardens and drinking Old Ben. In a large field at the rear, cock fighting, wrestling matches and other old time sports were regularly carried on. It is believed that the house derived its name from the fact that a hole was made in the wall through which pots of beer could be handed to customers outside. The photograph was taken in 1907, a few years before it was pulled down.

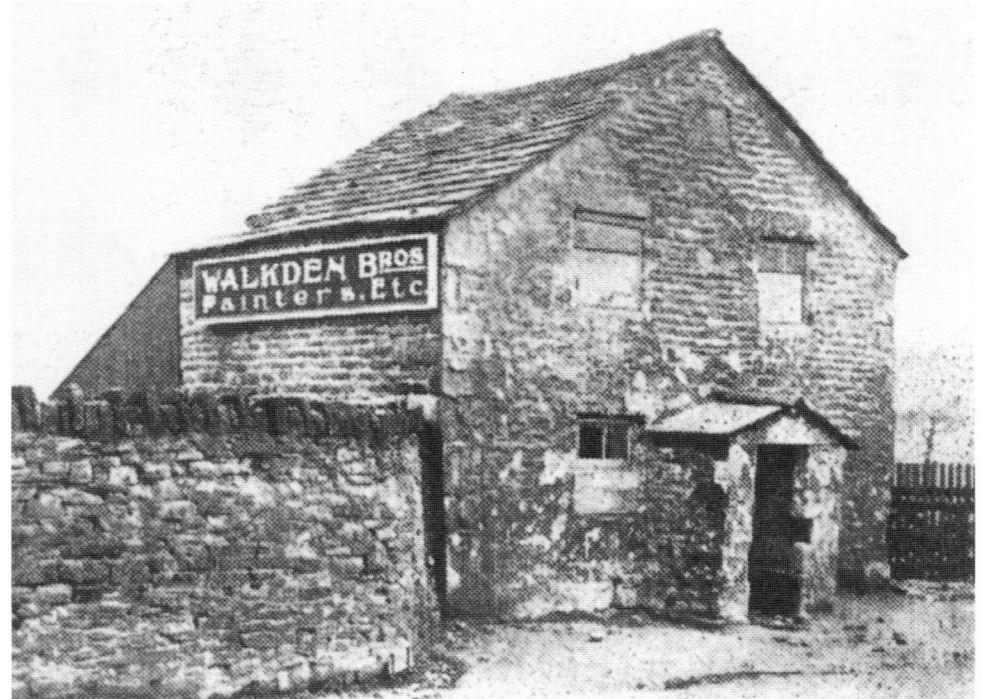

ERECTED FIFTY YEARS AGO
May 21st 1932.

Few people pass along Northgate, Salford and Griffin without noticing the drinking troughs placed there to meet the needs of thirsty animals.

Two of these conveniences were erected 50 years ago, when there were many more horses on the roads than is the case to-day. In grey granite, they were the gift of Mrs. Braybrooke, and bear the following inscription:-

"Erected and presented to the town by
M. E. Braybrooke, 1882. 'Be ye merciful',
for blessed are the merciful"

The one now in Northgate first stood at Sudell Cross near the *"big lamp"*, but subsequently was removed to its present position to leave a clear course for the increasing traffic. The Salford trough, at the junction of Cicely Lane, occupies its original place.

Sixteen years later, in 1897, Mr. James Carter was the donor of the red granite trough at Griffin, which is inscribed:-

"A righteous man regardeth the life
of his beast." Presented to the town
for the use of our dumb friends by
James Carter.
'He prayeth well who loveth well both
man, bird and beast'"

The photograph shows the Salford trough.

DANGEROUS ORNAMENTAL ARCH
August 13th 1932.

Queen's Park is to lose a landmark by the decision of the Town Council to demolish an attractive ornamental arch which covers the entrance of the park from Shadsworth. The substantial stone pillars and gates are to remain, and probably when the financial stringency is not pressing, steps will be taken to erect some new structure. The archway is being demolished because it is considered by the Borough Engineer to be in a dangerous condition.

As a jubilee memorial Queen's Park was opened on June 20th, 1887, to commemorate the reign of Queen Victoria. At that time the enclosure consisted of 33 acres. The total cost, including the ornamental lake, entrance gates, planting of trees, etc. was £15,000. This low expenditure was partly due to the generosity of landowners. The Borough Engineer responsible for the original plans was Mr. J. B. McCallum, and the mayor at the time was Mr. E. Appleby, who, along with the mayoress, planted oak trees in the enclosure to mark the occasion. It is recorded that 20,000 people witnessed the inaugural proceedings. At that date the ornamental lake and the entrance gates in question had not been constructed. The latter became possible by the generosity of Councillor Oddie and other gentlemen in the gift of the necessary land. A historian of the time recorded that on the opening day it was possible to see from the entrance in Queen's Park Road as far as Pendle Hill, Longridge Fells, Bleasdale Fells, Revidge, Billinge Hill and Hoghton Tower. As to the arch to be demolished, it is not known exactly how it originated, but it is believed that the stone was removed from another part of town - some say Ewood Park, as at that time this enclosure was used for trotting competitions.

WITTON WESLEYAN JUBILEE

August 27th 1932.

The Jubilee of Witton Wesleyan Church, Griffin Street, which was opened in 1882, is to be celebrated by a series of special gathering, commencing next Saturday with a reunion, to be followed on Sunday (September 4th) with Jubilee Services, conducted by the Rev. A. W. Wardle, of Accrington, a former minister of the church.

The foundation stone of the church was laid on May 28th 1881, by Mr. William Shaw, of Witton, and the building was opened on Thursday September 14th, 1882, by the Rev. W. T. Radcliffe, of Manchester. According to a report which then appeared in "The Blackburn Times", the edifice is a classic structure in the Italian style of architecture, and was built from designs made by Mr. G. Woodhouse, of Bolton. It cost £3,000.

Previous to 1868 there was no Wesleyan place of worship in Witton. About that time a room over a shop in Witton Parade was rented, and under the ministry of the Rev. W. Faulkner, the congregation increased rapidly and the room was always filled to its utmost capacity.

When the removal from Witton Parade took place the furniture consisted of but a few forms, a table, and a small harmonium. The mothers' monthly teas were commenced as far back as 1869. An event that cast a deep gloom over the members was the loss of £458 in a bank smash. A day school was opened and subsequently closed, a minister's house was purchased, an organ was installed in the church in 1891, and in 1902 the new school was opened.

COB WALL HOUSE
November 5th 1932.

Cob Wall House was built by James Fisher Armistead, who had inherited a large portion of his uncle's estate. He was the only surviving son of Thomas Armistead, of Blackburn, Calico Manufacturer, who lived at the house now numbered 44, Ainsworth Street, and occupied as offices by Mr. Henry Whittaker, Solicitor, and Clerk to the Blackburn Health Insurance Committee. James Fisher Armistead was born in that house in 1827. His father died when he was six years old, and he was brought up by his uncle, James Fisher, at Larkhill.

In 1850 or 1851 he married Emily Wingfield, a Lincolnshire lady, and, after his marriage lived for 18 months at Red Hall, Bracebridge, Lincolnshire.

Coming back to Blackburn, he lived in Princes Street, next door to Dr. William Cort, and thence went to Blackpool, where his eldest daughter was born.

Finding it desirable to reside in Blackburn in order to look after his estate, he purchased the houses shown on Gillies' map and reconstructed them (1854-56) to form Cob Wall House, and four of his children were born there. Mr. Armistead was a County and Borough Magistrate, and was noted for his kind heartedness in the administration of justice.

When it was proposed to build a new church for St. Michael's, Daisyfield, he repeated his uncle's offer to give a plot of land, and offered a site for the new church in Moss Street, but the Hornby influence was too strong, and the new St. Michael's was built in Whalley New Road, Brookhouse, adjoining the Hornby schools. Mr. Armistead died in 1905 aged 77 years. His wife predeceased him by five years.

Cob Wall House was occupied on lease for a period of six years (1860-66) by William Birtwistle, one of the pioneers of the cotton trade in Cob Wall district. It is now a Liberal Club. Across the Blakewater, close by, was Church Hill and Little Harwood Hall, the ancient manor-house.

MONTAGUE STREET CHURCH CLOSES

August 19th 1933.

A little later than usual, a small band of people straggled slowly out of Montague Street Congregational Church on Sunday evening. The door was locked. The last sermon had been preached, the last hymn sung, the last communion held.

After nearly 70 years service to the community Montague Street Congregational Church was closed, its struggling career ended. There was a suggestion to seal its fate a few years ago, but the closing was withheld. Now it is felt it is inadvisable to prolong further the efforts to keep the church alive. This decision was taken a little more than a fortnight ago; there is a debt of about £200. The question of the disposal of the buildings is at present in the hand of the trustees. Arrangements have been made for the children to attend other Sunday Schools, and the adults will no doubt attach themselves to other churches.

A small band of people from the Park Road Church, under the leadership of the Rev. West Pearson, started the church in 1862. Whit-Monday of the following year saw the laying of the foundation stone by Lord Teynham, and the building accommodating 700 people was opened in 1864. When the Rev. John Morgan accepted an invitation to the pastorage in 1868 he and his small congregation had to face a debt of £2,000 which by the end of 1874 had been entirely removed. A couple of years later the present galleries were added and other improvements carried out at a cost of £1,000. Structural alterations and the installation of a two manual organ cost £1,300 in 1889, and as a portion of that cost still remained a debt in 1902 a bazaar was held in the Exchange Hall which raised £640 towards the clearance of this and other liabilities.

The final services were conducted on Sunday by Mr. J. S. Roberts, who for some years has been Lay Pastor in charge. There were practically 100 at both afternoon school and evening service, and about 60 members remained for the communion service which marked the end of the church's existance.

ROSEHILL MILL
November 11ᵗʰ 1933.

In this mill on Higher Barn Street, Messrs. James and W. E. Briggs carried on business as cotton spinners and manufacturers for many years. At the beginning of the First World War (known as the Great War), it was worked by the Audley Ring Mill Ltd., but the spinning mill has been closed ever since. The last tenants of the weaving shed were the Queen Street Mill Co. (Darwen) Ltd.

It now stands empty and less than two years ago its weaving and preparatory machinery (393 broad looms) were sold piecemeal by auction. There is a stone tablet over the boiler house in the mill yard, but its inscription is now illegible.

The mill was originally built 1860-61 by Willan and Mills, machinists of Rosehill Foundry. Willan and Mills never worked the mill but leased it out to Messrs. J & W. E. Briggs.

ABBOTT CLOUGH TURNPIKE
January 12th 1935.

Though road tolls have long been abolished in Blackburn district, several of the old toll-houses still remain. One of the latest to be dismantled is the landmark on the Accrington Road near the Mother Red Cap Inn, just outside the Borough boundary. As will be seen from the picture, it has already been partly taken down. Its disappearance will allow a welcome widening of what is a very busy thoroughfare.

The last toll bar to be abolished in this area was at Shackerley, Preston New Road on November 1st 1890.

BLACKBURN CATHEDRAL SCHOOL

February 9th 1935.

HIGHER GRADE SCHOOL JUBILEE.

Prior to the erection of the Cathedral School there was no day school connected with the mother church of Blackburn.

The Sunday School was held at Bolton Road Station. The foundation stone of the school in Darwen Street was laid on April 25th, 1870, by the Bishop of Manchester [Dr. John Fraser]. Mr. Frederick Robinson, of Derby, a member of the Robinson family of Clitheroe Castle, was the architect, and the contractor was Mr. Edward Lewis. The estimated cost was £3,500.

In the summer of 1871 it was opened as a Sunday School, the scholars being transferred from Bolton Road Station; and in September of that year an elementary day school was started. Mr. Nicholas Taylor was the first head master. The school opened with 22 boys, 15 girls and 20 infants, but the numbers increased rapidly. On Monday, February 23rd, 1885, it was opened as a higher grade school.

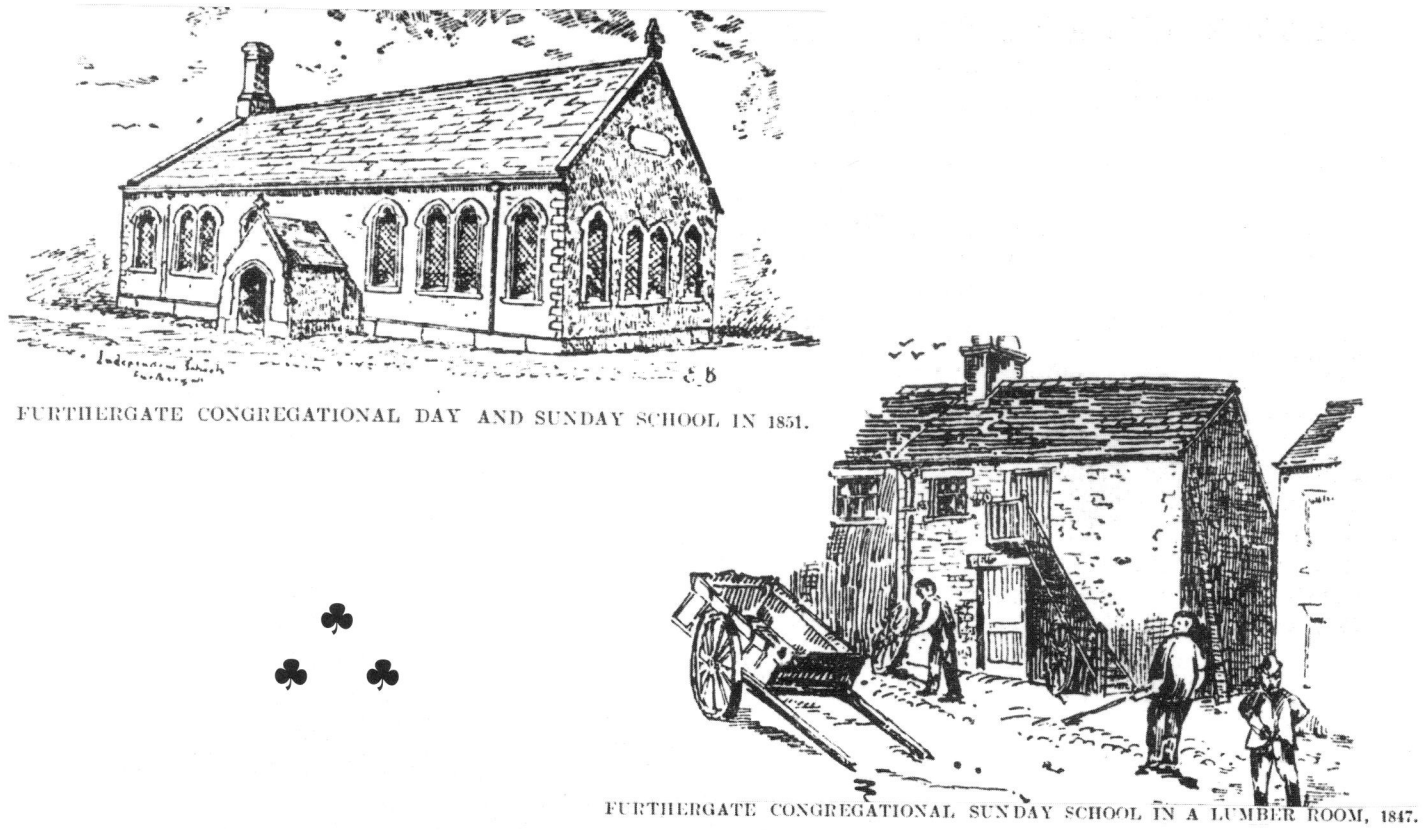

FURTHERGATE CONGREGATIONAL DAY AND SUNDAY SCHOOL IN 1851.

FURTHERGATE CONGREGATIONAL SUNDAY SCHOOL IN A LUMBER ROOM, 1847.

FURTHERGATE CHURCH
April 20ᵗʰ 1935.

There was a congregational mission at Furthergate, carried on in an upper room over a wheelwright's shop, approached by an outside wooden staircase. The rent was 1s-0d. per week. That was in 1847, and in 1851 a new school building was opened at the corner of Harwood Street and Bottomgate.

Furthergate Schools are situate near the eastern border of the town, where the turnpike roads come in from Burnley and Accrington. They stand at the corner of the main road with Harwood Street, locally known as *"Shade Loyne"*. Near the end of Shade Lane, where it crosses the canal, there were half-a-dozen large cotton mills in 1854, when the school was built, and some of them were there in 1847, when the school was started over the wheelwright's shop.

The district has grown marvellously since then, and Furthergate School and Church have been its principal religious, social and educational centres. The present schools were enlarged in 1863, 1882, 1894 and 1907, and other buildings have grown up around them.

BIT OF OLD WITTON
January 11th 1936.

Four humble cottages in old Buncer Lane now in course of demolition provide a link with the days when Witton was a hamlet of Blackburn. They were built in 1834, four years before St. Mark's Church, which they face, was consecrated.

In the hollow between flows the River Blakewater. The wall on the right of the photograph is part of the old wall which enclosed Witton Park, before the new Buncer Lane, which cuts through the park, was made. The old lane was nothing more than a cinder path which skirted this wall, and was the only road from the south side of the river to the church on the rising ground on the north bank. A footbridge, still there but not now used, spans the river at the foot of the wall.

It was over this bridge and up the lane which leads to Witton Stocks that some of the tenants of these cottages saw a man running; and whose evidence was an important link in the chain of evidence which led to the conviction and execution of Cross Duckworth for the murder of the little girl, Alice Barnes, in November 1892.

The stone stocks were only a few hundred yards from these cottages. On a map for 1848 they are shown on a spot which is now marked by the footpath in front of Mr. George Mayor's shop. There is little sentiment attached to the disappearance of this old property. They have no backyards or modern conveniences other than gas and water.

COAL MINING IN BLACKBURN

February 8th 1936.

Coal has been mined in Blackburn since Queen Elizabeth the First's days. Coalpit Moor was the site of numerous small pits, and is near the extremity of the rocky spur called Whinney Edge, which slopes down rapidly towards the River Darwen at Ewood. What is left of the moorland is dotted with the remains of old coalpits, and the Blackburn Corporation Hospital is built in the midst of them.

On the 26th of January, 1846, Charles Haworth, a rising young Blackburn artist, made a pencil sketch of one of the abandoned collieries on this moor. The framework of the pithead is seen to have been both primitive in structure and rickety in condition, but it had been used to wind coal up a vertical shaft from a depth of about fifty feet, and the winding was done by horse-power. The shaft, with the crossbar to which the horse was harnessed, is seen in the pencil-sketch, resting on the ground and supporting the great horizontal wheel, which apparently would have fallen down without this prop.

"Coalpit Moor", alias "Whinney Edge," was one of the three several wastes, moors, or commons, belonging to the rector and the lord of the manor of Blackburn, which were enclosed and divided between them and a few others in 1618. The cluster of coalpits on this moor, together with many other clusters in Livesey, Tockholes, Lower Darwen and Over Darwen, indicate the position and extent of the South Blackburn Coalfield, which covers several square miles of land at the extreme south end of Blackburn Parish.

OLD WITTON
January 21st 1938.

This picture depicts a row of old cottages at Witton Stocks, facing the Infant School. The houses in the background are the backs of the houses on Selbourne Street, and in the gap between the cottages and the houses, can be glimpsed Buncer Lane and the trees of Billinge.

(On the ordnance survey map of 1937, the cottages are shown with no street name, but it is certain that the postal address was simply Witton Stocks. - J.H.)

THE SITE OF SAMLESBURY AERODROME

February 24th 1939.

A view of picturesque cottages on the lane from Myerscough and Balderstone which will soon be in the hands of demolition workmen to prepare the site for the new aerodrome at Samlesbury. The houses are in the proximity of the proposed assembly factory shortly to be built.

Another old farmstead to be sacrificed in preparing the site is Collins Farm, Balderstone, which is quite an old and interesting building, but never-the-less it has to go in the sake of progress.

MONTAGUE STREET BAPTIST CENTENARY
March 17th 1939.

A reunion of past and present members and friends of the Montague Street Baptist Church will be held to-morrow to celebrate the centenary of the church, which was formed in March, 1839, with nine members.

The Montague Street Church was formed under the guidance of the Lancashire and Cheshire Association of Baptist Churches. Rooms were rented in Ainsworth Street and services commenced there on Good Friday, March 29th, 1839. Although the members were limited they were so full of faith and courage that under the guidance and promised help of the Association they entered immediately upon a scheme for the building of *"The Tabernacle"*. So successful and determined were they that they saw their new church opened on Good Friday, April 17th, 1840.

For many years it had been felt that a new church was needed, and it was decided to proceed with the work. The last service in the Old Tabernacle was held on Sunday, April 3rd, 1910, and on April 30th the same year the foundation stones were laid of the present church, which, with furnishings cost £6,000. The building was opened on May 11th, 1911.

OVERLOOKERS HALL SOLD TO BREWERY

May 19th 1939.

Blackburn has lost many old and cherished institutions, mostly as a result of trade conditions. Following meetings of the Blackburn and District Overlookers Association it has been decided to dispose of the finely built Overlookers Hall in High Street to Dutton's Blackburn Brewery, Ltd., to enable that firm to carry out a scheme of office and administrative extensions.

Since last Friday meetings have been held in various parts of the district, and as a result of the vote the committee have been authorised to dispose of the hall and site to the brewery company. The purchase price has not been divulged.

The Overlookers Hall was opened on May 6th, 1911, by Mr. Joseph Bullon, the president, who had the support of Mr. A. H. Gill, M.P., and Alderman A. Smith. M.P. The association membership at that time was 1,500, representing 130,000 looms. The present-day membership is 930. It is a matter of regret that these very convenient premises should no longer be available, especially in view of the fact that four years ago the Overlookers Association celebrated its centenary.

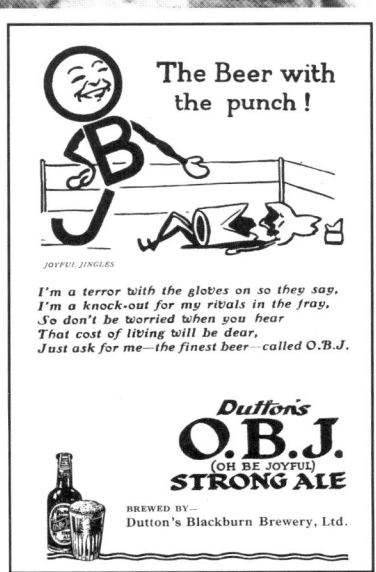

UNDERGROUND SHELTER

September 1st 1939.

There were scenes of busy activity in various districts of Blackburn yesterday when a number of emergency schemes to provide protection to the population in the event of war were inaugurated. The Corporation made a start with several projects which are not likely to be completed for several days. These include emergency shelters for the public, provision for school children and so forth.

The photo in this article shows the process of sand-bagging at Salford by Messrs. Dutton, brewers, who have available a very commodious cellar under the site of the old offices and buildings of Messrs. Shaw and Co, which has now been cleared. It is estimated that several hundred employees can be housed here should the emergency arise. The only indication to the cellar is the door shown in the picture, and the protecting sand bags.